What Leaders Are Saying

"This is an excellent resource to help believers identify their spiritual gifts in the context of the small group. This book also equips small group leaders to mobilize each member to exercise his or her spiritual gift. Read this book and watch your small group come alive!"

Pat Robertson, chairman & CEO, Christian Broadcasting Network; host, *The 700 Club*

"Nothing can bring vibrancy and life to a small group more than each member discovering, developing and using his or her spiritual gifts. This timely book is a practical roadmap showing you how to get there and how to activate your full potential for ministry. I encourage you to read it and to use it!"

C. Peter Wagner, chancellor, Wagner Leadership Institute

"Throughout history the renewal of the Church has been triggered by the rediscovery of God's promise in Acts 2: 'I will pour out my Spirit on all flesh. . . .' This work will guide its readers to the recognition of that reality as an essential factor in small group ministries—one of the most effective means of outreach in our postmodern era."

Paul E. Pierson, senior professor of history of mission, Fuller Theological Seminary

"Once again Joel Comiskey has shared a book that will help to shape the cell churches in the generation to come. His insights are fresh and biblical!"

Ralph Neighbour, founder, TouchGlocal

"Joel Comiskey has again provided the Body of Christ with an important tool to see God's Kingdom revealed in and through small groups. If the Holy Spirit's presence, empowerment and gifts do not infuse life into the group, it becomes nothing more than a Gospel gimmick for church growth. *The Spirit-Filled Small Group* is a must-read for every pastor or leader desiring to see first-century Christianity restored in the 21st century."

Chuck Crismier, founder, Save America Ministries;
radio host, *Viewpoint*

The Spirit-Filled SMALL GROUP

Leading Your Group
to Experience
the Spiritual Gifts

Joel Comiskey

 CCS Publishing

www.joelcomiskeygroup.com

© 2009, 2016 by Joel Comiskey

Published by CCS Publishing
23890 Brittlebush Circle
Moreno Vally, CA 92557
1-888-511-9995

Printed in the United States of America

Library of Congress Cataloging-in-Publication Data
Comiskey, Joel, 1956-
    The Spirit-filled small group : leading your group to experience the spiritual gifts / Joel Comiskey.
        p. cm.
    Includes bibliographical references (p.   ) and index.
    ISBN 9780984311002 (pbk.)
    1. Church group work. 2. Small groups. 3. Gifts, Spiritual. I. Title.
BV652.2C644 2005
    253p.7—dc22   2005009888

To C. Peter Wagner,
my mentor and model in ministry,
who has inspired me to think beyond the box

CONTENTS

INTRODUCTION

Small group resources tend to overlook the spiritual side of small group leadership. And yet most would agree that spiritual preparation is the most important aspect of leading a small group. Only God's supernatural power can draw people to the truth and liberate them to be all that God wants them to be. Only through the Spirit's power can we expect to see the miracles that Jesus talked about when He said that if we would abide in Him, we would bear much fruit and even do greater works than He did while He was on earth.

What excites me most about small group ministry is the intimate home atmosphere in which God has the perfect opportunity to change people's lives, prepare them for ministry and further His Kingdom work. I have seen this happen over and over in my own ministry.

At the age of nineteen, I was a zealous Christian (I had accepted Christ two years earlier), living in Long Beach, California, when God spoke to me that I would soon be leading a home Bible study. Several weeks later, my brother Andy, a brand-new believer, approached me about leading a small group made up of friends who were freshly converted from Satan's domain. We met together every Friday night either at my parents' house or next door at our friend Gloria's house. Our agenda for those meetings was simple: We just wanted God.

I made many mistakes while leading that group. At that time, I thought that "Spirit-filled" meant I did not need to prepare for the lesson, but that I could simply open my mouth with the hope that God would fill it. Needless to say, it was a time of learning and growing!

Despite my weaknesses, God's Spirit, combined with His Word, transformed our small group's atmosphere. We became best friends. The gifts of the Spirit flowed during each meeting, reminding us that He was alive and working among us. At times forty people would gather, but most of the time, there were the "core" fifteen young people gathered in my parents' house week after week.

One week, Ginger Powers, a missionary involved in smuggling Bibles to Eastern Europe, spoke to our group about missions. As she spoke about God's compassion for a lost world, I felt God's clear calling on my own life for missionary service. Months later, I joined Youth With A Mission, which focused on outreach in Canada. Soon after, I enrolled in a Canadian Bible school with the goal of starting my missionary career after my graduation. Although the small group stopped meeting regularly, we did reunite during Christmas and summer breaks to share our common bond.

During that time, God sparked a love in my heart for small group ministry, a love that continues to this day. My wife, Celyce, and I served as missionaries in

Ecuador from 1990 to 2001, before returning to become missionaries to North America. Small group ministry has been the full-time focus of my research, writing and ministry for the last thirteen years. My wife and I lead a weekly small group in our home and have even started a small group-based church in Southern California called Wellspring. At this point in our lives, we could not live without small group ministry.

The Distinction of This Book

The key distinction of this book is the spiritual perspective it gives to small group ministry. So much of the literature about small groups that is already published relates to small group technique and only touches briefly on the Spirit's power. This book is a practical reference guide to help small group leadership begin to move in the supernatural realm.

The book's first priority is to help small group leaders and members trust the Holy Spirit to lead them, empower them and work in their group. Small group facilitators often sense a lack of guidance, power and spiritual authority. Jesus knew His disciples would be powerless without a touch from the Holy Spirit, and so He told them to wait in Jerusalem, saying, "You will receive power when the Holy Spirit comes on you; and you will be my witnesses in Jerusalem, and in all Judea and Samaria, and to the ends of the earth" (Acts 1:8). Small group leaders need a power boost to make small group ministry relevant and exciting.

The second priority of this book is to help the facilitator identify and mobilize each small group member to use his or her own spiritual gifts. Small group facilitators often feel ill-prepared to identify spiritual gifts of the people in the group. I firmly believe that the small group atmosphere is the perfect place to develop the gifts of the Spirit in each member's life, and so it is essential that the facilitator know how to do this.

A pastor friend of mine once encouraged me to discover how spiritual gifts work in the small group. He lamented that no material existed specifically on that subject. To help meet his need, he hired a spiritual-gifts expert to come to his church to teach his small group leaders about spiritual gifts. It is my prayer that this book will not only help small group leaders identify spiritual gifts but will also help pastors encourage the usage of spiritual gifts throughout the small group ministry.

Spirit-Led Small Groups

George Barna points out that 37 percent of the members of Pentecostal and charismatic churches attend small groups during the week, as compared to members of Baptist (22 percent) or Methodist (15 percent) churches.[1] Because the membership is higher among Pentecostal and charismatic churches, it can also be assumed that more leaders are raised up to facilitate groups among those in the charismatic camp.

Without a total dependence on the Holy Spirit's work, small group ministry does not work well—and it normally turns into a burdensome task. Lawrence Khong, pastor of a 10,000-member small group-based church in Singapore, notes, "I would unequivocally state that without moving in the life and power of the Spirit, it would be impossible to have a dynamic cell church. . . .

Cell members without the Spirit's power would burn out from demands of the cell structure. . . . True body life is experienced only when members give room for the work of the Spirit and know how to minister to one another with the Spirit's anointing."[2]

Whatever denominational or non-denominational label a church wears, the most important characteristic, in my opinion, is promoting individual sensitivity, devotion and dependence on the Holy Spirit. In a Holy Spirit-charged atmosphere, cell leaders are best raised up and members are encouraged to minister in their giftedness.

Some churches are better at empowering lay people than others. Those that are less adept often make lay people feel they must possess a theological degree (much like the pastor has) before they can successfully minister to a small group. The emphasis in such churches is on acquiring *Bible knowledge* rather than *obedience* to Scripture and *dependence* on the Holy Spirit. In such churches, a high premium is placed on sitting and hearing the Word preached each Sunday. While I agree that small group leader training is essential, ultimately the graduate must step out and depend on the Holy Spirit. And my observation is that success in small group ministry will hinge on that dependence.

Effective small group leaders and churches emphasize the Holy Spirit's empowerment in daily life and the fact that all believers are priests and ministers of the living God. Such churches emphasize the need for each member to depend on the Holy Spirit to guide, direct, empower and even take the biblical text and apply it to daily experience. It is this atmosphere that makes small group ministry work successfully—whether the church is Baptist, Methodist or Assembly of God.[3]

A Description of Small Groups

Small group ministry must involve more than sitting in a circle and hearing someone preach a sermon. It must involve the ministry of every member actively applying the Word of God to daily life. The definition of a *small group* that I will be using in this book—and the one followed by the majority of worldwide small group-based churches is this: "a group of three to fifteen people who meet weekly outside the church building for the purpose of evangelism, community and discipleship, with the goal of group multiplication."

This definition offers a great deal of flexibility with regard to homogeneity, lesson material, the order of the meeting, the location of the meeting and degree of participation. Yet the definition maintains key quality-control characteristics.

Admittedly, many other types of groups exist in a church, including boards, committees, the choir, Sunday school groups and prayer groups. While the principles in this book will apply to all such groups, I am writing primarily to those leading or attending weekly, outreach-oriented, multiplying small groups—as described by the above definition.

I use the generic term *small group* in this book because of the vast variety of titles and names given to groups. Some of the churches I work with use names such as *heart groups, life groups* or *cell groups* to describe their small groups. The term *small group*, therefore, applies to a wide variety of names.

Who Should Read This Book

This book has been written for those who are leading (facilitating) a small group, participating in a small group or considering joining a small group. I use the word *leader* with some reservation because of its connotation of position and power. In some cultures, for example, a leader is a person who controls and dominates. Many people believe that a "Christian leader" automatically holds an official position in the church. A new consensus, however, has developed that defines the word *leader* with one word: *influence*.[4] When I use the word *leader* in this book, I am referring to a person who exercises his or her God-given capacity to *influence* a specific group of God's people toward God's purposes for the group.[5] I often interchange the word *leader* with *facilitator*, because the best small group leaders encourage participation by the members of the group.

Although this book has primarily been written to prepare small group leaders to operate in the power of the Spirit, the subject matter will touch all group members, because all are involved in making the supernatural a reality in the context of the small group life. Group members should read this book for two particular reasons: First, members make a significant contribution to the life of the cell. Each member will be intimately involved in causing supernatural events to happen—using the gifts, intercession, etc. In the life of the group, no one is to sit back and do nothing. The best cell leaders, in fact, rarely "lead" the entire cell, instead encouraging cell members to participate actively. Second, members are the next in line to actually lead the small group.

I am assuming that the readers of this book are believers who desire God and are seeking to walk in the Spirit. I am also assuming that those reading this book are studying the Bible and growing in their relationships with the Lord.

Topics Not Covered in This Book

Most small group-based churches have established a training process that prepares a group member to become a small group leader. I will not be talking about such a training track in this book; however, I have dedicated an entire book to that subject because I do believe that training is essential.[6] In this book, however, I will assume that the small group leader or member either has or will receive church-sponsored training in such topics as doctrine, devotional life, evangelism and small group dynamics.

Nor will I cover the general topic of small group dynamics—the art of leading a small group. I have already done that in my book *How to Lead a Great Cell Group Meeting* (Touch Publications, 2001). In that book, I wrote about the order of a meeting, facilitation, transparency, asking stimulating questions, listening, encouragement, reaching out to non-Christians, small group stages and the many other details of a small group.

There are many great books dedicated to defining each spiritual gift in detail.[7] Many other authors cover gifts beyond the scope of this book, such as voluntary poverty, hospitality, celibacy, missions, exorcism, martyrdom, artistic creativity, craftsmanship and music. Rather than cover every possible gift, this book will focus on how the Spirit uses gifts in the small group context and guides the leader to facilitate a Spirit-filled group. Because this book is written to lay leadership rather than senior leaders of the Church, I will not cover in detail the five-fold offices that Paul mentioned in Ephesians 4.[8] Instead, the gifts I will cover in this book are explicitly listed in Scripture (the one exception is intercessory prayer, which I call a spiritual gift although some would disagree).

To remain effective in small group leadership, I recommend that each small group leader have a coach. This coach might be the senior pastor, a staff pastor or another volunteer lay leader (for example, the leader of the mother cell that gave birth to the new cell). I will not cover the discipline of coaching, nor the small group coaching structure necessary to have long-term success. I have covered the theme of small group coaching organization, as well as the other topics mentioned here, in other books.[9]

Let's now begin our study of how spiritual gifts work in the small group.

Part I

Spirit-Filled LEADERSHIP

1

THE FILLING OF THE SPIRIT

For two years, I lived in Pasadena, California, the home of the famous New Year's Day Rose Parade. One year during the parade, a beautiful float suddenly sputtered and coasted to a halt. It was out of gas. The whole parade was held up until someone could get a can of gas over to the float and get it moving again. The amusing thing was that this float represented the Standard Oil Company! Even with its vast oil resources, the company's truck had run out of gas.

In much the same way, Christians often neglect their spiritual maintenance, and although they have been filled with the Holy Spirit, they need to be refilled. When the greatest evangelist of the nineteenth century, D.L. Moody, was asked why he said he needed to be filled continually with the Holy Spirit, he replied, "Because I leak!" Like Moody, we all run out of gas and need the power of the

Holy Spirit to recharge our lives. This chapter will clarify how to be filled continually with the Holy Spirit.

The Power of the Holy Spirit

In Ephesians 5:18, Paul wrote: "Do not get drunk on wine, which leads to debauchery. Instead, be filled with the Spirit." In the original Greek, the phrase *be filled* is a present-tense verb. To signify a "one-time filling," Paul would have used the past tense or a future verb tense; instead, he chose the present tense to denote that the filling of the Holy Spirit is *not* a one-time event, but a continual experience. Scripture says that we must be continually filled with the Spirit, not just once or twice.

The word *filling* seems awkward when referring to the Holy Spirit's entrance into our lives. The Spirit of God is not a liquid, like water. He does not fill a person the way cold milk fills a cup. The Holy Spirit is God—He is one in essence with the Father and the Son—but He is also a distinct Person and has all the attributes of a person. That is why we refer to the Holy Spirit as the third Person of the Trinity. Many Scripture passages point to these facts. [1] Like a person, the Holy Spirit searches, helps and guides.[2] He knows; He feels; He wills. Scripture speaks of the Holy Spirit's mind, His love and His instruction.[3] In Ephesians 4:30, Paul wrote: "Do not grieve the Holy Spirit of God, with whom you were sealed for the day of redemption." The only way we can grieve someone is if the one we are grieving is a person.

Because the Holy Spirit is a Person, it makes more sense to talk about the Holy Spirit's *control* or *compulsion* in our lives, rather than His *filling* of our lives. *Holy Spirit-driven* is a good way to look at our response to His control. A person who is filled with the Spirit is driven by the Spirit—driven in a gentle, loving way. A Spirit-driven person allows the Holy Spirit to direct and guide every decision, plan and activity. Because the world, the flesh and the devil oppose the Spirit-controlled lifestyle, we need to be filled and renewed continually.

I was first filled with the Holy Spirit in early 1974. In September 1973, approximately four months earlier, I had received Jesus by praying the prayer of salvation in my bedroom, yet I lacked power in my life. During those initial months as a Christian, I was afraid to pro-claim to others my newfound faith in Christ. I was in my last year of high school and desperate to become bold about my faith. My lack of spiritual power led me to attend a miracle service of Shekinah Fellowship that gathered in a Foursquare church in downtown Long Beach, California.

Although I responded to the general altar call after the service, I knew exactly what I needed. I longed for power and boldness so that I would not be ashamed of my Christian faith. The elders at Shekinah prayed for me to receive the fullness of the Holy Spirit. I knew that they hoped I would immediately receive the gift of tongues as a sign that the Holy Spirit had fallen upon me.

I did not speak in tongues that night, but change was evident the very next day. My mom and I went to Pastor Chuck Smith's church, Calvary Chapel, in Costa Mesa, California. All I could do was talk about Jesus—I witnessed about Jesus to everyone I saw that day. I even grilled my mother repeatedly about her faith. (She graciously over-looked a lot of zealous behavior in those days!)

My life was totally transformed from that night on-ward. I began to carry my Bible with me everywhere, setting it down on the right corner of each classroom desk at Millikan High School. I wanted people to know that I was a believer—and I had the confidence to prove it. The Shekinah Fellowship experience, however, was not enough. I needed repeated fillings of the Spirit's grace and power.

Later, I did speak in tongues: I stepped out by faith and spoke in an unknown prayer language to God. Speaking in tongues was not a grand emotional experience for me, but it has helped me greatly during times when words cannot express my yearnings and petitions to God. I am thankful for the gift of tongues.

Some would call what happened to me at Shekinah Fellowship that night in 1974 "the baptism with the Holy Spirit." Other would classify it as Joel Comiskey's "first filling after conversion." The most important point, however, is that I desperately needed His fullness in 1974, and I need it just as much today. I believe that my first filling in 1974 was not sufficient—it was only the first in a long line of subsequent encounters with the Holy Spirit.

Even in the book of Acts, those who experienced the Pentecostal outpouring with tongues of fire in chapter 2 still needed a fresh wind of the Holy Spirit in chapter 4. Only *two* chapters later, those same apostles prayed to the Lord and the place was shaken: "And they were all filled with the Holy Spirit and spoke the word of God boldly" (Acts 4:31).

It seems to me that our debates over terminology have often prevented us from seeking the Spirit's continual fullness. All Christians can come together under the banner of eagerly desiring the Spirit's fullness, even though not all believers label that experience in the same way. Craig Keener, a Southern Baptist professor at Eastern

Seminary who had an experience of Holy Spirit similar to my own, said:

> If we could get past some semantic debates in our discussions about the timing of the baptism of the Holy Spirit, we would have more time available for the more practical questions surrounding the Spirit's empowerment. Nearly all Christians agree, for example, that all Christians have the Spirit by virtue of being born again. We also agree that we all should regularly experience a Spirit-filled life, walk in the Spirit, depend on the Spirit's power in our behavior and witness, and be open to experiences from God's Spirit subsequent to conversion.[4]

Before leading a small group seminar for Southern Baptist missionary leaders in Prague, Czech Republic, in 2003, I was approached by one of the missionary leaders who told me: "The only way to reach Eastern Europe with the Gospel is to seek the fullness of the Holy Spirit and operate in all of the gifts of the Spirit." This missionary leader understood that heathen, demonic forces are too powerful for us to minister effectively apart from yielding completely to the Holy Spirit's working. He wisely guarded his terminology, but he was speaking the same language that I hear repeatedly around the world. This Southern Baptist missionary wanted what other hungry believers across Christendom have desired throughout the ages: the power and fullness of the Holy Spirit's presence in life and ministry.

The Power of Prayer

I heard about a particular church whose electric organ stopped halfway through the hymn singing during Sunday morning worship. The organist was not sure what to do. Fortunately, the pastor was in control of the situation, and he asked the congregation to follow the Scripture reading, intending to lead them in prayer as well. As he read the Scripture portion, an usher quietly approached the organist and handed her a note that read: *The power will be on after the prayer.*

The power comes on after prayer! The Scripture makes it crystal clear that God is exceedingly willing to fill us with His Holy Spirit. All we need to do is pray. Jesus taught His disciples that the heavenly Father would freely give the Holy Spirit to anyone who would simply ask (see Luke 11:13). But Jesus was not content to talk about the Holy Spirit on just one occasion. Over and over throughout the gospels, Jesus incited expectations among His disciples about the promised Holy Spirit. He would be a comfort, a guide and a teacher who would remind them of everything Jesus had spoken (see John 14–16).

Some people who speak or write about the Holy Spirit convey a burdensome message of human effort in order to obtain the Spirit's fullness. Their message, whether intentional or not, emphasizes that "we have to *depend*," "we have to *be filled*," "we have to be *sensitive*." Such focus stirs me to turn inward rather than outward on the wonders of the Holy Spirit.

I believe one hundred percent that God expects our clear-cut human response, yet the process should not be burdensome or heavy. I read one book on the Holy Spirit that made me feel as if the Holy Spirit would depart immediately if He were in any way "offended"—even in the slightest way. After reading the book, I found myself fearful of making even the smallest mistake, thinking that the Holy Spirit was flighty and easily quenched. Once again, I felt that it all depended on *me*.

I now believe that the opposite is the truth. It is my understanding from Scripture that the Holy Spirit is eager, willing and excited to work in us and flow through us—even though we are frail, weak human beings.

Ask and you shall receive! I do not know a better, more effective way to be filled than simply asking for the Holy Spirit's fullness. The power comes on after the prayer. I am not aware of even one incident in the Bible in which God did not pour out His Spirit on those who sincerely asked.

God granted Elisha his request when he asked for a double portion of the Spirit (see 2 Kings 2:9). God answered Solomon's request when he cried out for the Spirit's wisdom to lead the nation of Israel (see 1 Kings 3:7–9). Jesus clearly said that our loving heavenly Father will freely give to His children the Holy Spirit (see Luke 11:13). Jesus repeated over and over throughout the gospels the Father's willingness to answer our prayers (see John 14:13–14; 15:7; 16:23–24). The good news is that the Spirit longs to control our lives—and this is especially true when it comes to facilitating a small group. As you prepare for your own small group, ask Him to fill you and control you. And He will.

Some people set up long lists of dos and don'ts that must be completed before God will give His Holy Spirit. While some of those suggestions are commendatory (such as the confession of sin and a commitment to obedience—see Acts 5:32), long lists often give the false appearance of an unwilling God who is playing hide and seek with His people.

27

I am writing this book to small group members and leaders who aspire to minister in the context of the small group, and thus I am assuming a longing for holiness and conformity to scriptural truth. But my point is that we will never be "good enough" to receive the Holy Spirit. As my Old English paraphrase says, "There is none that doth not sin!" You fail, just as I fail. Do confess any known sin, and do eagerly desire obedience. But don't stop there. Ask Him boldly to fill you, and He will. The Spirit knows that you will run out of gas without Him. Your small group leadership, in fact, *depends* on the Spirit's control and direction in your life. Pray that He will fill and control you. He will.

The Holy Spirit's Willingness to Fill Us

After the Spirit descended at Pentecost, churches were formed throughout the Mediterranean region. Most of them received the Holy Spirit as a gift of grace and continued growing in Christ. Some, like the Galatians, slipped back into legalism. The apostle Paul rebuked the Galatians for not maintaining the simple faith—walking with the Holy Spirit. Paul wrote: "I would like to learn just one thing from you: Did you receive the Spirit by observing the law, or by believing what you heard? Are you so foolish? After beginning with the Spirit, are you now trying to attain your goal by human effort?" (Galatians 3:2–3).

The Spirit of God flowed freely among the Galatians as long as they related to the Holy Spirit on the basis of faith and freedom. In the beginning, the Galatians rejoiced in the Spirit's fullness as a pure, free gift of faith. Yet when the Galatians fell captive to the human tendency toward good works and legalism, the Spirit took a backseat and no longer freely moved among them. The Spirit moves through us on the basis of grace and faith.

One of the greatest hindrances to small group leadership is forgetting that the Holy Spirit wants to fill us, bless us, produce His fruit in us and operate His gifts through us. Our chief work is to allow Him to do so. First Corinthians 2:12 should be universally memorized: "We have not received the spirit of the world but the Spirit who is from God, that *we may understand what God has freely given us*" (emphasis added). One of the principal ministries of the Holy Spirit is to reveal to His children those things that the heavenly Father wants to give us freely.

This is especially true for small group leaders who are faced with the extra challenges of pastoring and caring for God's flock. The demonic realm works overtime to discourage small group leaders—because of the importance of their work.

The need is great for small group facilitators to receive refreshment and bask in His love and grace. Small group leaders need to take time to listen to God's wonderful plans for the gifts and blessings He wants to pour out on them and through them.

Our Need to Receive His Fullness

Once we realize how much the Holy Spirit wants to bless and fill us, we need to spend time in His presence in order to receive His fullness again and again. I believe in this strongly and wrote an entire book on the subject of quiet time spent in His presence.[5] I strongly urge each cell leader and member to spend quality time each day for devotional prayer, worship and meditation on God's Word. I believe the daily quiet time is the most important discipline of the Christian life.

In addition to daily devotions, small group leaders should spend time with God before the small group starts. Before the small group meeting, allow God's fullness to thoroughly drench you, until you sense His fullness of joy and exceedingly great riches. Allow Him to infiltrate your mind, your attitude and your emotions. Psalm 16:11 declares: "You have made known to me the path of life; you will fill me with joy in your presence, with eternal pleasures at your right hand." The natural result of spending time in God's presence is joy and peace.

More than lesson preparation, small group success depends on the leader's personal spiritual preparation. A statistical investigation of three thousand small group leaders demonstrated that the leader's personal spiritual preparation was far more important than time spent in preparing the lesson material.[6] It is a mistake, in fact, to think that anything is more important than the leader's spiritual preparation before the group starts (such as refreshments, lessons, a vacuumed rug). Remember the story of Mary and Martha—Christ's positive response to Mary demonstrated that the most important item on our agendas is time spent with Him. Basking in God's presence will fill you with the power, insight and confidence necessary to lead your group to new heights.

During this alone time, be sure to read the Word of God. Meditate on a passage that stands out to you. In the process, you will feed yourself, and others will notice the difference (see 1 Timothy 4:16). Listen to God's voice: He will show you how to pray for each member of the group. Above all, seek God's face and He will fill you with His Holy Spirit. Ask the Spirit to control you both at that moment and during the meeting. Begin to experience His joy. You need the Spirit's overflow in your life to be able to bless those in the group. They will see God's presence in your gaze, your love and your anointed authority.

If you can, do yourself the favor of spending one or two hours in His presence before the small group starts. Even if time is scarce, *make* the time to spend thirty minutes in soul preparation. Your group will be glad you did. For those leaders who are employed fifty or sixty or seventy hours per week and find it difficult to spend time in Christ's presence before the small group meeting, understand that the Holy Spirit knows the intention and desire of your heart. He is willing to take you where you are and fill you on the spot. Just ask Him. Don't fall prey to guilt or condemnation.

Satan, the accuser of the brethren, is only too quick to unload deadly darts. But God's grace is always sufficient, and He will work with you where you are. Remember Psalm 32:1–2: "Blessed is he whose transgressions are forgiven, whose sins are covered. Blessed is the man whose sin the LORD does not count against him." Then verse 7 expresses the psalmist's faith, with God's response stated in verse 8:

> You are my hiding place; you will protect me from trouble and surround me with songs of deliverance. I will instruct you and teach you in the way you should go; I will counsel you and watch over you.

The Real Power Source

In 1972, NASA launched the exploratory space probe Pioneer 10. The satellite's primary mission was to reach Jupiter, photograph it and its moons and then beam data to Earth about the planet's magnetic field, radiation belts and atmosphere. Scientists regarded this as a bold plan, because until that time no satellite had gone beyond Mars. Pioneer 10 far exceeded the expectations of its designers, not only zooming past Mars, but also Jupiter, Uranus, Neptune and Pluto. By 1997, 25 years after its launch, Pioneer 10 was more than six billion miles from the sun. And despite the immense distance, the satellite continues to beam back radio signals to scientists on earth. How does Pioneer 10 continue to emanate signals? The eight-watt transmitter. The key to the continual success of Pioneer 10 is its power source.

The power of Pentecost is available for all believers today, including you, and especially you! Your job of leading a small group is very significant because you are pastoring the Church of Jesus Christ. You are intimately involved in transforming the lives of those for whom Christ died. And your group is God's instrument to help lost people find their way to God.

Your Spirit-filled participation will add life to Christ's Body. The Holy Spirit is available to fill, guide and pour out His grace. Just ask.

2

Living in the Spirit

I have been married to my wife, Celyce, for nearly eighteen years. I thought I knew her when we walked down the aisle of the Long Beach Alliance Church in 1988. But I now realize that I hardly knew her back then. It has taken eighteen years to uncover who Celyce really is and how I can best relate to her. I have grown in my love for Celyce over these eighteen years. I have also been challenged on how insensitive I can be. Since I am the only male in our household, surrounded by Celyce and three daughters, the need for sensitivity is even greater!

Growing in our walk and sensitivity to the Holy Spirit is what the Christian life is all about. Walking with the Person of the Holy Spirit is an exciting adventure, but it also takes time to learn who He is, what He likes and how to please Him.

A Focus on His Power

One lesson I have learned about the Holy Spirit is that He does not request, require or even want our self-sufficiency. He receives the most glory, in fact, when He is in control, not us. When we are the weakest, He is the strongest. Often in those very moments when we feel the most frail, disoriented and unsettled, the Holy Spirit has the greatest opportunity to manifest His strength, power and creativity. The Holy Spirit longs for us to cling and to cry out to Him. When we are strong, we do not usually feel the need or desire to do so. But our helplessness creates the opportunity for us to jump into His arms.

Throughout the Old and New Testaments, we see a God who searches for vessels that will look to Him and give Him glory. God had to take away the fighting forces of Gideon, for example, so that he would not boast in his own strength. When God whittled Gideon's army down to three hundred men and the odds of human victory were reduced to one hundred percent impossible, God told Gideon to go ahead. And as always, God came through in a miraculous way (see Judges 7).

God gave Paul revelation after revelation, but he eventually became so puffed up that God could not use him any longer (see 2 Corinthians 12:7). To remedy the situation, God gave Paul a "thorn in the flesh"—a painful trial—so that Paul would keep his eyes on God alone. Even though Paul pleaded with God to remove the trial, God refused, saying, "My grace is sufficient for you, for my power is made perfect in weakness" (2 Corinthians 12:9). Paul concluded:

> Therefore I will boast all the more gladly about my weaknesses, so that Christ's power may rest on me. That is why,

for Christ's sake, I delight in weaknesses, in insults, in hardships, in persecutions, in difficulties. For when I am weak, then I am strong.

2 Corinthians 12:9–10

Paul wrote that God has chosen people who are weak, foolish and despised in the world's eyes, so that His glory would be acutely manifested and everyone around would immediately recognize the grace and power of God. It is clear throughout Scripture that God wants all the glory (see 1 Corinthians 1:31).

If you as a small group facilitator feel weak and inadequate, you are in the right place! Your weakness is the Holy Spirit's opportunity to glorify the Father. Rather than plead with God to remove your insecurity, ask God to receive glory through it. God loves to use weak small group leaders who look to Him rather than to themselves.

One of my heroes is a woman named Lorgia Haro. Back in 1995, Lorgia agreed hesitantly to host a small group. The leader of the group she attended was moving, and I practically pleaded for someone to host the group while we searched for another leader. Lorgia slowly raised her hand, but she shared her feelings of inadequacy due to her timid nature and the fact that her husband was not a Christian.

Lorgia fulfilled her commitment and opened her house. Unlike Lorgia, we did not fulfill our commitment—we never did find a leader for that group! In the absence of anyone else to lead, Lorgia stepped up to the plate. She asked for the Holy Spirit's strength before each meeting. Her shyness forced her to depend on God's strength, and through her weakness, Jesus used her to love people into the Kingdom. The group grew.

35

As she grew in confidence of the Holy Spirit's power, she encouraged members to facilitate their own groups. "If I can do it," she reasoned, "you can, too!" Within the space of seven years, her group multiplied twelve times and more than seventy people received Christ. Her husband was one of those converts. Our church grew tremendously because of one weak, shy woman named Lorgia Haro.

Mikel Neumann, a professor at Western Seminary, studied small group leaders around the world and noticed the same pattern. He concluded that the Holy Spirit specializes in using weak, dependent people. In his book *Home Groups for Urban Cultures,* Neumann writes about two leaders:

> They had started three or more groups, and the leadership seemed a bit puzzled. The woman was exceptionally shy, and the man had trouble expressing himself. . . . I was impressed that it is not outstanding speaking gifts that bring a new home group into existence. Caring and prayer . . . are the keys to starting new groups. These leaders allowed other people to participate, recognizing that others had gifts that needed to be used.[1]

It is my guess that the two leaders in Neumann's study discovered the Holy Spirit's energy at their point of weakness—shyness and faltering speech. Scripture tells us to look to the Lord and seek His face always (see Psalm 105:4–5). I have noticed repeatedly that small group leaders who feel weak in themselves but cling to God's power are the most effective. These leaders realize that apart from God's strength, they have nothing to offer the group.

The Spirit's Anointing over Information

Great small group leaders stay informed. They are constantly reading and growing in their knowledge. They study and meditate on God's inerrant Word—and they live by it. They are also familiar with the art of small group dynamics. They value lesson preparation and are mentally prepared when small group night arrives. But I have also detected a danger in this pursuit: Some leaders come to depend on knowledge and information—as if it replaces the Holy Spirit's guidance.

So many unexpected things happen in the course of a normal small group: members arrive late, babies scream, guitar strings break, Mr. Talkative is in an even more talkative mood than usual—and has brought along a chatty visitor. Prepackaged plans offer little help for real-life small group situations.

Great small group leaders depend on the Spirit's wisdom and direction. Information, plans and preparation help, but they are insufficient. It is Spirit-anointed common sense that grants success and helps a leader make decisions on a moment-by-moment basis. Jesus said that the Holy Spirit would bring back Christ's words to our memory. The Holy Spirit would grant comfort, counsel and guidance. The Spirit longs to grace the Church with His gifts and to see people changed, healed and eager for more of Him.

The apostle John warned the first-century believers not to seek special knowledge (Gnosticism) from the mystery teachers who supposedly had arrived at a higher level of spirituality. Rather, John told them:

As for you, the anointing you received from [God] remains in you, and you do not need anyone to teach you. But as his

37

> anointing teaches you about all things and as that anointing is real, not counterfeit—just as it has taught you, remain in him.
>
> 1 John 2:27

Each believer already has the God of the universe dwelling inside! While God has raised up teachers in the Church, the greatest Teacher, the Holy Spirit, lives within you!

Ask the Holy Spirit to bring back to your remembrance lesson nuggets during the meeting. Remember that you have an eternal listening device plugged into your ears at all times. If you depend on Him and listen willingly to His voice, He will show you what to do during the small group meeting. He will guide you. When the meeting starts, cling ever so lightly to your preconceived plans and depend confidently on the Holy Spirit to guide the flow—wherever He might take you.

Technique and small group dynamics might be the most important aspects for non-religious small groups. Christian small groups, however, are distinct. God is the main attraction. The Spirit energizes all members to participate according to their gifts and talents. Knowledge and information, while important, take a backseat to the Spirit. God the Father whispers direction to the small group leader through the Holy Spirit. His anointing teaches before, during and after the small group. We must allow Him to work in us and to give us the victories that we so desperately need.

My own group decided to rotate into someone else's home, and I had asked a trainee to lead the group. I dreaded going that night. My mind was in so many different places, and I certainly did not need another meeting. But the Holy Spirit showed up. Jesus was there in the worship. Everyone could sense His presence. Several people shared impressions they were getting for the group through the gift of prophecy. Praise and gratefulness flowed to God's throne as people acknowledged the Holy Spirit's manifesting Himself through the gifts of the Spirit. The facilitator applied God's Word, allowing us to freely answer the open-ended questions. The leader moved out of the way sufficiently to allow for free-flowing conversation. One of the members revealed during the application of God's Word that he and his family were facing a crisis and a possible move to Tennessee. The leader felt the Spirit saying that we should lay hands on this couple, and God ministered both to them and to us. After a group walk around the neighborhood doing prayer evangelism, we shared refreshments together. As I ate a delicious chocolate-chip cookie and engaged in fellowship, I thought to myself, *I'm glad I came tonight!* When the Holy Spirit is present, He always makes small group ministry exciting.

When we wait on God and He fills us and strengthens us, a renewal takes place in our own hearts. The Spirit births clear leading within us, and we can hear His voice in a clear way. The Spirit of God leads the way, and then He shows us the way to go.

Information leads to transformation. The anointing of the Spirit turns a weak facilitator into an anointed vessel. God gives the leader the power to make it happen, and everyone acknowledges Christ's presence.

Gentle, Peaceful Impressions

The Holy Spirit speaks to us in a peaceful way. Paul declared in Colossians 3:15: "Let the peace of Christ rule in your hearts, since as members of one body you were called to peace. And be thankful." The phrase *rule in your hearts* means to make the calls, much like an umpire calling a game. God's peace will help us know His decisions for our lives, just as an umpire calls balls or strikes. God speaks in His peace. There is never turmoil. His voice is always surrounded with sweetness and life.

When learning to listen to the Holy Spirit's voice both in and outside the small group context, the same rule applies. The Holy Spirit speaks most often through gentle impressions that are accompanied by peace.

He impresses His gentle, peaceful voice and thoughts through gentle nudges. We can never be one hundred percent sure, of course, that God is speaking; we can only be one hundred percent sure that God's written Word is without error as originally given. But we *can* come to the place where we more accurately hear God's loving voice.

Learning to hear His voice is a process that takes a lifetime to fully develop. Even though Jesus said that His sheep will hear His voice (see John 10:3–4), we must also realize that lambs have to *learn* to recognize their shepherd's call. It is a process. It takes practice. And God might never speak to you exactly as He spoke to Samuel or Elijah.

We can be confident, however, that we will grow in hearing God's voice the more we walk with the Spirit and spend time in His presence. We will perfect a listening ear the more we spend time with God in secret. As we spend time with the Maker, He will speak to us more often and more clearly, and we will receive divine guidance that will transform not only our own lives, but also the lives of those around us.

When God speaks to my own heart, it is hard to describe exactly how I know He is speaking. I simply know because His impression is clear, gentle and right. My inward reaction is, *Yes, that's it.* These impressions might show me whom I should call, where I should go or what I should do.

Even when God is speaking to us about sin, He comes in a direct yet tender way. By contrast, Satan disrupts, disturbs and causes turmoil. He is a thief, a murderer and a liar who shocks, causes grief and loves to leave people helpless and confused.

God's Voice	Satan's Voice
• Accompanied by peace • Gentle wisdom • Freedom • Power to accomplish the task	• Accompanied by fear • Confusion • Pressure • Guilt because of the difficulty of the task

When you are in the midst of a cell meeting and you sense confusion, condemnation and fear, rebuke it, because that is not of God. When God's gifts are flowing freely through members, confusion will cease. In His presence, there is rest, fulfillment and comfort. I am not saying that there will never be conflict. But the goal is to work through the conflict until Christ's peace reigns once again.

The Bible tells us that the "kingdom of God is . . . righteousness, peace and joy in the Holy Spirit" (Romans 14:17). God's voice is without fear and without doubt. It is a voice that is gentle, loving, kind and considerate. It is always good, it never brings turmoil and it always leads us down the right path. It always has our best in mind—even through the trials. God wants no harm for His children.

While studying in Canada, I was approached by a troubled and fearful fellow student who said, "I woke in the middle of the night and felt God say to me, *Prepare yourself to die.* I feel so fearful. Do you think that God spoke to me?"

"No way," I told him. "God wouldn't provoke fear in you. Rebuke the devil."

I knew from experience that God does not scare us with His will. I agree with Everett Lewis Cattell:

> I heard another helpful thing from some preacher. He said that . . . whenever we were seized with a sudden impulse to do something odd and to do it quickly, we could be practically sure that the impression had come from the devil. . . . This has proved true in my later experience. God is love; He does not give us guidance as a form of punishment but rather as a loving expression of His interest in the affairs of our lives.[2]

Hearing His voice will always involve something good, something beautiful. Scripture tells us that every good and perfect gift is from above. Only the perfect ones come from heaven. James 1:16–18 states very clearly:

> Don't be deceived, my dear brothers. Every good and perfect gift is from above, coming down from the Father of the heavenly lights, who does not change like shifting shadows. He chose to give us birth through the word of truth, that we might be a kind of firstfruits of all he created.

We need to seek God's peace when hearing His voice and moving in the gifts of the Spirit. The Christian life is full of trials and difficulties, and the absence of hardships is not necessarily a sign that God is present. But I am talking about something deeper—that peace that surpasses understanding and outward trials. In John 16:33, Jesus said: "I have told you these things, so that in me you may have peace. In this world you will have trouble. But take heart! I have overcome the world."

The Spirit's Blessing for Each Member

The Holy Spirit delights to work in the lives of each member of your small group. God's will for each group member's life is just as important as God's perfect will for your own life. I recommend not only that you pray for each member of your small group but that you also dream about—consider, contemplate—God's will for each one of them. Paul said in Philippians 4:8:

> Finally, brothers, whatever is true, whatever is noble, whatever is right, whatever is pure, whatever is lovely, whatever is admirable—if anything is excellent or praiseworthy—think about such things.

We often apply this verse personally, but it also works well to apply it to the members of the small group.

Start by dreaming about the Holy Spirit freely pouring out His grace, fruit and gifts on each member. Then think about how you as a leader can be a channel of the Holy Spirit to fulfill God's wonderful plan in each life. Think about the great works God wants to do. As you begin to envision God's plan and purpose for each group member, you will be able to see beyond talkative Tom and conflict-driven Connie to His plan of transformation for them. You will see afresh how God wants to use you as His channel to heal their lives.

Human nature is selfish. We tend to think of ourselves before anyone else. When thinking of God's will, our human tendency is to meditate on God's will for our own lives. Yet God has a perfect plan and will for each believer on the face of this earth—including those members who are attending your small group.

Perhaps Michael is studying to be a doctor. Donna may feel called to raise children as a full-time housewife. Judy works outside the home and then rushes home in the evening to care for her kids. Toni just received Christ and is still struggling with alcohol. These are just some of the activities of the group members, but what is it that *God* wants to perform in each of their lives? What is His perfect plan for them? This is a huge question—the most important one. And it is the one that you, as the small group leader, are called to answer.

Ask the Holy Spirit to reveal His plan for each group member's life. Dream about those plans as the Holy Spirit gives them to you. The Holy Spirit wants to use you in some way to help each person fulfill God's will. You will have to get to know them personally before those dreams and plans make sense. But it is important to begin.

Holy Spirit–Directed Praying

Prayer is Holy Spirit language. It is the way we communicate with God—and the way He communicates with us. In Ephesians 6:18, Paul wrote: "And pray in the Spirit on all occasions with all kinds of prayers and requests. With this in mind, be alert and always keep on praying for all the saints." Prayer is the most important ministry a small group leader can use to work in harmony with the Holy Spirit for the good of the group.

When the facilitator begins praying for a group member, God begins to work in that person's life in a powerful way. Prayer transforms the leader's relationship with that member. Through prayer, the healing balm of the Holy Spirit breaks the strongholds of bitterness and unforgiveness. A oneness develops through the bonding power that prayer creates. Paul wrote: "For though I am absent from you in body, I am present with you in spirit and delight to see how orderly you are and how firm your faith in Christ is" (Colossians 2:5). It is possible, and important, to be present "in spirit" with someone through prayer.[3]

My questionnaire of seven hundred small group leaders in eight countries revealed that prayer for group members was the leader's most important way of unifying and strengthening the group in preparation for multiplication. Those small group leaders who prayed daily for group members were twice as likely to multiply their small groups than those who only prayed occasionally.[4]

John, a small group leader in Melbourne, Australia, noticed that one of his small group members named Mark had developed a rotten attitude and was even vocalizing it. John dedicated himself to praying daily for Mark, even sending cards of appreciation to him and his family.

Week after week, the walls slowly crumbled. One day, John called Mark's office and was told that he was sick and at home. During his lunch break, John visited Mark, praying for him and giving him a big hug before leaving. Mark broke down and confessed his mean spirit and selfishness. He gave John full permission to speak into his life. Today they are best friends; Mark is even a cell leader now, under John, and is doing very well!

Through prayer, barriers are broken down and relationships are healed. A new spiritual bond develops that establishes intimacy and oneness. Prayer gives God the liberty to work in a new way.

I encourage small group leaders to tell their group members, "I'm praying daily for you." This statement develops a spiritual relationship between the leader and members. The most important gift you can give someone is the gift of prayer. It is a gift that lasts and that continues to bear fruit throughout eternity.

Along with praying for members in private, I encourage cell leaders to pray aloud for them during meetings. As Marjorie, for example, prays for each member during the meeting, her pastor's heart is evident. Her prayers are specific and personal, yet she does not reveal confidential matters. She warmly lifts each person in the meeting before the throne of God. Marjorie knows her flock, and they are willing to follow her. This type of prayer tells members that their leader cares for them and desires to minister to their needs. It is also an excellent way to model intercessory prayer.

Marjorie's example encourages everyone to press on in the Lord in prayer. Because she paid the price in intercessory prayer, she was able to meet the needs of those around her. She connected with the group immediately and met the needs of each member.

Once you have prayed for someone during the week in your own quiet time, it is easy to pray later for the person in public. People will notice the oneness that you have with that person, and God will come through and meet every need.

Part 2

Spirit-Filled GROUPS

3

Worship and the Word
in Spirit-Filled Groups

D on't teach about worship as part of the small group order when you're speaking to our leaders," the pastor told me right before the seminar started. "We don't practice worship in our small groups. It's too much of a hassle to train the leaders to direct worship, and after all, our small groups are primarily for non-Christians."

"Okay," I said, nodding outwardly while wrestling inwardly with this revelation. I was surprised to learn that the typical small group in the church excluded worship, particularly on the basis of sensitivity toward nonbelievers. They were missing an important means of evangelism, along with other workings of the Spirit.

While I strongly believe that small group ministry is a powerful tool to reach the lost, we must first give our attention to the Almighty. While techniques to lasso non-Christians are great, they are not at the core of small group ministry. God must be at the core. Worship is the atmosphere in which God lives, and His Word expresses who He is. When a group is God-sensitive, it highlights worship and the Word. In this atmosphere, the gifts flow and unbelievers are naturally drawn to Jesus.

Jesus said, "Worship the Lord your God, and serve him only" (Matthew 4:10). Worship first; service second. This order is repeated later on in Matthew when Jesus said: "'Love the Lord your God with all your heart and with all your soul and with all your mind.' This is the first and greatest commandment. And the second is like it: 'Love your neighbor as yourself'" (22:37–39). The gifts of the Spirit flow when God is exalted and given the place He deserves. In this God-centered atmosphere, unbelievers are converted.

The Normal Focus of a Small Group

The normal cell group, like a good diet, includes certain staple ingredients. I recommend the following ingredients in all small groups:

- *Upward focus:* Knowing God through worship and prayer
- *Inward focus:* Knowing each other through fellowship
- *Outward focus:* Reaching out to those who do not know Jesus through small group evangelism

- *Forward focus:* Raising up new leaders through training and discipleship

No two small groups are exactly alike, but each should include these four ingredients. UIOF (upward, inward, outward, forward) is a great way to view the progress of a small group. The UIOF focus provides good general direction, which can then be acted on specifically. My own small group, for example, uses four *W*s as guidelines: welcome, worship, the Word and witness (or works).

The icebreaker (*welcome*) touches some area of the past, and though it is often humorous, it reveals a lot about each person. *Worship* draws the members into the presence of the living God. The small group lessons (the *Word*) avoid the impersonal, one-man-show mentality and ask each person to contribute. Finally, the vision-casting time (*witness*) requires group involvement—working together to win a lost world to Christ.

Worship and the Word are central elements of any small group. The Spirit's gifts flow in, around and through these times. Let's take a closer look.

Worship from the Heart

Worship is an intimate experience that is supercharged with group strength. When other believers are lifting up their voices to the throne room, God is glorified and His Body is energized. In such an atmosphere, transformation takes place.

Worship can make the difference between a dynamic cell and one that stumbles along without strength to stand firm. We need to see Jesus in a new way, and this will take place when God's people worship together. Worship opens

51

the way for everything else to happen. Worship clears the air—it takes the victory from the devil. We should never hide from worship; it is absolutely essential in small group ministry. Worship is the strength that holds us up and keeps us growing in Him.

Praise Leads the Way

Jehoshaphat had a problem. As king of Israel, he was commissioned to protect his nation. Yet a vast army from Edom was camped on his doorstep, ready to destroy the nation of Israel. Jehoshaphat's immediate response was natural alarm and fear. Yet he also took the right next step: He sought after God and proclaimed a fast throughout Israel. As the entire nation waited before God, the Spirit of God came upon Jahaziel, son of Zechariah, and he prophesied to those present, "Do not be afraid or discouraged because of this vast army. For the battle is not yours, but God's" (2 Chronicles 20:15).

What kind of battle plan did God give the nation of Israel? A worship plan! The story continues:

> Jehoshaphat appointed men to sing to the LORD and to praise him for the splendor of his holiness as they went out at the head of the army, saying: "Give thanks to the LORD, for his love endures forever." As they began to sing and praise, the LORD set ambushes against the men of Ammon and Moab and Mount Seir who were invading Judah, and they were defeated.
>
> 2 Chronicles 20:21–22

God still works mightily through worship today. Worship ushers in an atmosphere in which the gifts of the

Spirit can operate. When God's people praise and worship Him, God shows up and begins to speak through His gifted body.

In the midst of worship, prophecy and praise, the Spirit comes and brings life, power and peace. The Spirit can give us the strength we need to meet the great and grave needs around us.

When we worship in our small groups, God shows up. He blesses. He makes us alive. He does great things. At times, I feel so weak when I am leading my cell group. Yet as we worship, God always shows up. He comes to the group. His life is manifested among us. God moves in a special way and brings a special peace.

Without Christ's presence, the cell group is no different from a work party, a family gathering or a meeting of friends at a football game. Even if non-Christians are in attendance, Christ's presence is often what the non-Christian really wants. Nonbelievers who attend a small group frequently want to know and experience the reality of God. Some have called this worship evangelism; it is the idea that as we lift Jesus high, He will draw all people to Himself. Referring to His death, Jesus said, "But I, when I am lifted up from the earth, will draw all men to myself" (John 12:32). We need to face the fact that only God can draw someone to His presence.

Children Join In

Many intergenerational/family small groups allow children to stay in the small group during worship, but they then leave during the Word time for their own small group lesson. Children often bless the small group with simplicity and clarity and remind adults that worship is

53

not complicated. In my opinion, children supercharge the small group atmosphere during times of praise and worship. Some people think that children are a distraction, but I have found that just the opposite is true. Children reflect Christ's nature and often draw others into His presence. And the side benefit is that children grow through watching their parents worship in a small, Spirit-filled environment.

I try to encourage children to understand that God loves them and wants to hear their praises to Him. At times, during the music portion, I like to stop and remind them of the words of a song or even ask them to pray.

The Ministry of Music

Many leaders feel inadequate to lead times of worship because in their minds, they feel that they have to play the guitar or worship like Matt Redman to lead God-honoring worship. I have experienced worship times in which the members choked out a joyful noise (and I do mean *noise*). Due to lack of guitar talent, some groups play a tape or CD, while the members follow along. I think this is a great idea, and we have done it in our own group on occasion. God doesn't require a tabernacle choir. He looks at our heart motivation as we sing to Him.

Normally, the worship leader should pick five to six songs before the group begins. I encourage the leader to type the words of these five or six songs on a piece of paper and then distribute those song sheets to everyone in the group. Those who know the songs won't need the sheets, but many others will. Or the worship leader might invite group members to select the songs before the worship time and then sing them in sequence.

It is a good idea for the small group leader to give an exhortation to begin the worship time. One particular leader used to say, "Remember that God is looking at your heart. Reflect on the words of the songs while you're singing and know that above all else, you're pleasing God." I have discovered that a simple exhortation like this makes a huge difference in the atmosphere.

It is a good idea to intermingle times of silence during and after worship songs. Both during and after worship, allow time for people to pray out loud. Allow God to speak a prophetic word to the group. So often in Scripture, God manifested His presence through worship, and it is vitally important to hear from Him during this time.

In one meeting, the leader concluded the lesson time by playing a CD of worship songs and asked the members to remain in silence as the Holy Spirit ministered to them. The Spirit ministered to our souls as we just sat before the Lord for ten to fifteen minutes, and we left that time supercharged with joy. Several parents who were stressed due to demanding kids and schedules were especially touched. The worship time energized us to serve each other. Dynamic talk and fellowship characterized the remaining moments of that night.

Remember, singing is an important part of worship, but it is not the only activity. At a small group seminar, one participant shared this: "It's important to go beyond singing songs. Our group has experienced God's presence through reading psalms together, praying sentence prayers or even waiting in silence."

Beyond the songs themselves, worship is an experience of drawing near to God and allowing God to draw near to us. It is more than simply music; it is coming before the living God with all of our hearts and seeking His face. It is loving Him with all of our hearts and wanting Him above all else. Our inward motivation is critical to worship. Only God can break down the pride and carnality of a hardened heart. The worship experience tenderizes the hearts of those who are about to hear His Word, and He begins to work mightily in the lives of those who hear. It is God's Word that makes this possible.

God's Inerrant Word

During the sharing of the Word in the small group (normally after the worship time), God speaks to our hearts through the Bible. Many small groups follow the same theme and Scripture passage as was used in the Sunday-morning message. Even if this is the case, it is best *not* to discuss what the pastor said on Sunday. The people should interact with God's Word, not with the sermon, which is merely the words of one human being. The reason is simple: If the sermon itself is the reference point, visitors and those who missed the celebration service will feel isolated. They will feel inhibited in freely participating in the group.

The Word and the Spirit

Remember that the Word and the Spirit go hand in hand. There is a lot of truth in the oft-repeated phrase, "Without the Spirit of God, Christians will dry up, but without the Word of God, believers will blow up!" Both the Spirit and the Word are essential. God wants to use both to transform His Church through the small group. He uses the Word to keep us on track, but the only way we can apply the Word of God is through the Spirit of God.

For a number of years, one of my group members attended a church that believed all supernatural gifts ceased with the completion of the New Testament. As I got to know him, I discovered that he had been taught (and he believed) that the Spirit equaled the Bible. Subtly, he wanted to convert the small group into a Bible study, because for him, the Bible and the Spirit were one. He had little experiential knowledge of the Holy Spirit as a Person, working in and through the believer. When our group began a time of worship, I noticed that he struggled with seeking God and fully entering God's presence. We had to work long and hard with him, and in fact, I never thought he would stay. I was wrong. This young man was eventually touched by the Spirit's fire and the wonderful sense of community. He discovered a relationship with the Spirit, the Word and God's people that was life transforming.

The Spirit is very much alive, and He wants to apply the Word of God deeply into the recesses of our lives. Two key words in the Greek language are helpful to describe how the Spirit does this. One of these words is *rhema*, and the other is *logos*. The *rhema* word is God's living Word that dwells within us, whereas the *logos* is God's written, objective Word. God will never contradict His *logos* (written Word), but when the small group comes together and the Holy Spirit is moving, the *rhema* word will freely flow, bringing transformation.

Paul used the term *rhema* when he told the Ephesian Christians to take up the "sword of the Spirit" (Ephesians 6:17). He was referring to the indwelling words (within us through meditation and memorization) that believers are to carry around continuously and have ready to use at a moment's notice. The small group atmosphere is a perfect opportunity to allow the Holy Spirit to minister to one another through the *rhema* words stored inside the minds and hearts of believers. It is wonderful when God gives His people words of encouragement and blessing to edify each other in the small group.

God wants us to study and live by His written Word. But as we meditate and memorize His written Word, His *rhema* word begins to dwell richly in us. I encourage small group leaders to meditate on and memorize God's Word and then to allow the Holy Spirit to flow through them freely while they are facilitating the small group. A Scripture might come to your mind while facilitating the discussion. Boldly apply it to the group. Only the Word of God is able to transform the members' lives. The Spirit takes the Word of God and sets us free. Jeremiah said: "When your words came, I ate them; they were my joy and my heart's delight" (Jeremiah 15:16). As the leader meditates upon God's Word, the Spirit of God will make it living, powerful and sharper than any two-edged sword (see Hebrews 4:12).

God's Truths for Each Member

It is essential that small group leaders examine the lesson materials—even those provided by the church—and apply them according to the needs in the group. Whatever type of lesson material the small group facilitator uses, it should be based on the inerrant Word of God. Because all that we are and do in the Christian life must be guided and governed by God's Word, all the experiences, discussion and demonstration of the gifts of the Spirit should be based on God's Word. Gifts such as prophecy, the word of knowledge and wisdom, discerning of spirits, tongues and the interpretation of tongues must be judged and held accountable to God's Word. The Holy Spirit will never contradict what has already been written. He inspired the Bible once and for all. The Word must serve as a measuring line for all that we say and do.

The small group is all about applying the Word of God to daily life—not about dispensing information about the Bible or theology in general. People are inundated with information; what they need is transformation. The small group is the best place, for example, to wrestle with applying the truths heard in the sermon on Sunday. Questions can be asked, such as: How am I measuring up? What do I need to change in my life? How can I please God more?

This helps members learn to apply the teachings of Scripture, particularly when small groups feature accountability between members. Karen, a member of a small group I was leading, heard about the need to have a daily quiet time. "Would you hold me accountable to actually having one?" she asked the group. Karen could confidently ask this question because she knew we loved her. As a group we had repeatedly affirmed her desire to follow Jesus, even though Karen stumbled in her Christian life. And we did ask her about her quiet time at the next meeting and the following meeting after that. Later, Karen asked the group to hold her accountable to quit smoking.

I strongly believe that small groups are absolutely the best way to make disciples, to see real change take place in people's lives. In a large Sunday-morning gathering, it is easy to hide.

As I sat next to Nancy on the plane, she shared her testimony with me. She had received Jesus and begun attending a large evangelical church that faithfully taught God's Word each Sunday. "Over time," she said, "it became painful to smile, walk through the church doors, hear the message and leave one hour later to resume our family crisis in the car in the church parking lot." She finally stopped attending church because she felt like a hypocrite. For Nancy, going to church was equated with hearing the preacher on Sunday.

Applying the Word of God in the small group atmosphere helps people like Nancy—or families like Nancy's—to obey the Word. The Hebrew word for *obey* means "to hear." To truly hear God's Word implies obedience, as opposed to simply receiving information. James wrote: "Do not merely listen to the word, and so deceive yourselves. Do what it says" (James 1:22). The Greek word for *obey* literally means "to hear under." The idea of obedience in the New Testament is a hearing that takes place under the authority or influence of the speaker, thus leading to compliance with the teachings.

Jesus asked that His disciples "hear Him" to the point of complying with His requests. Often the disciples did not understand Christ's words or teaching. They failed to grasp the meaning of Christ's death on the cross (see Matthew 16:22), their own place in the Kingdom (see Mark 9:33–37) and humble service to others (see Matthew 20:24). They lacked the finesse and education that characterized the elite of that day. Yet Jesus must have noticed their humble commitment to trust and obey His teachings.

60

Knowledge without obedience does not cut it in the Kingdom. When Paul and Barnabas waited on the Holy Spirit in Acts 13:2–3, the Holy Spirit clearly spoke through the prophetic word: "Set apart for me Barnabas and Saul for the work to which I have called them." God separated them to the work of the ministry and did wonderful things through them. Paul and Barnabas obeyed and went. They did not know what the future held, but they obeyed and left. The Spirit is looking for people who will obey Him, and small group ministry highlights the application of the Word to the point of obedience.

Transparency

Effective facilitators encourage others to talk. I tell small group leaders to follow the 70/30 rule, which means allowing others to share 70 percent of the time while the facilitator talks only 30 percent of the time.

The facilitator normally prepares (or is given) three to five questions based on God's Word. These questions should promote open discussion among the members. A good rule of thumb in preparing these questions is to ask yourself each question beforehand and discern if you yourself could openly discuss the question—or can it be answered with just yes or no answers?

For people to share transparently about their own lives, the leader must begin with this type of transparency. Group members will typically be as transparent and open as the leader is willing to be. If the leader is not willing to risk transparency and openness, the members will certainly not step out.

As the leader speaks forth how God's Word has had an impact on his or her own life, many others will be encour-

61

aged to speak. The gut-level reality that great leaders take to the group is *essential* in order to make it work; people will then be encouraged to share how the Word of God applies to their daily lives. An atmosphere of transparency allows that to happen. David Hocking writes:

> Learn to admit your mistakes in the presence of the group and to apologize sincerely when things go wrong or do not turn out the way you expected . . . admitting failure in the midst of success is a key to good leadership. Learn to be open and honest before others. They'll love you for it (or at least fall over backwards out of shock!).[1]

If the leader always wants to give the best impression, the other cell members will do likewise. Some leaders imagine that they are promoting transparency, but their testimonies do not resonate with the members. "Pray for me," they might say. "I became slightly impatient with a fellow worker today. That's the first time I've ever had a conflict at work. Please pray." Testimonies like this close people off, causing them to think the leader is a super-saint, when in fact, that is not the case.

Transparency is also the best evangelistic tool to reach non-Christians. People without Christ appreciate authenticity. They are thankful when Christians share struggles, because often the non-Christian is going through situations far worse, but without Jesus to help. Cell evangelism is a very natural activity, and it penetrates the defenses of those who would never darken the door of a church building, but who need love and a sense of belonging.

Even if you do not have a major problem to share, you can still talk about the small, daily difficulties you face. We all struggle with long waits in line, unwanted calls, computer breakdowns, demanding work schedules and other irritations of life. Transparent sharing, however, does not involve sharing only difficulties. What about your desires and plans? Transparency means talking about yourself in an honest way, allowing others to know your aspirations, dreams and hopes.

The supernatural power of the Word comes through a supernatural touch on our daily lives. God's Word transforms us and makes us more like Him. The Word of God encourages us to press on and make it happen. It is amazing how God will use each member of the cell to minister to the others. God wants to use each person as he or she allows the Spirit to move.

Transformation

The grave need of time spent in the Word is to grab the hearts of the people. Great small group leaders are always looking for ways to apply the Word of God to the lives of the members. Some people share all of their struggles, but they have no intention of ever changing. Instead, they expect deep sharing to bring them a certain cathartic experience. While this may be helpful, only transformation will produce the desired result. The rest is temporal and could even be labeled emotional.

To increase transformation in the lives of members, some small group leaders conclude the Word time by saying: "In light of what we've read and discussed in this passage, how do you think God wants to use this in your life or the life of this group?"

It is great when the Spirit of God takes the Word of God and places a hook in the cleft of a member's heart. I am always honored when I see a small group member during the week who is still applying the biblical passage we discussed in the small group. One week, for example, I led the group in a discussion on 1 Timothy 4:12, in which Paul wrote to Timothy, "Don't let anyone look down on you because you are young, but set an example for the believers in speech, in life, in love, in faith and in purity." During that small group, the Holy Spirit applied Paul's teaching to our own lives—our families, work relationships and friendships. God spoke to us about exemplifying what we wanted others to follow. When I talked with Sunitha, one of our small group members, five days later, she said, "God is still speaking to me about how I need to walk in purity and be an example around the other teachers at the elementary school where I teach."

Sadly, many facilitators expound on a passage without ever grabbing the heart. People leave with information, but not true transformation. Even though the Word of God is living, powerful and sharper than any two-edged sword (see Hebrews 4:12), they keep God's Word at a distance, never allowing it to penetrate deeply. The Holy Spirit wants to take God's Word from our heads to our hearts.

I encourage small group facilitators to go for the jugular—life transformation through God's Word! The devil is not scared at all when a cell leader heaps on platefuls of information; but he trembles when God's Word causes members to put away idols, turn from sin and change their behavior. Grab the heart. Be sure that people are touched and transformed. Make certain that people have taken the Word and applied it.

The Spirit's presence in worship and His ministry in the Word create a powerful atmosphere in which the gifts can flow. The whole concept of the Spirit within us is powerful and riveting. It is exactly what we need to see great things happen in our midst. The power of God *will* manifest in our midst, but we need to trust Him to do it.

4

EDIFICATION IN
SPIRIT-FILLED GROUPS

John, a pastor in San Diego, California, who had been implementing small group ministry for several years, said to me, "Joel, I didn't know I had so many dysfunctional people in my church until we started small group ministry! It's as if I lifted up a wet log in a dark forest, only to see bugs scurrying everywhere." Those same needy people sat in Pastor John's church every Sunday wearing suits and ties, and outwardly everything seemed proper and in order. But as they began to interact with one another in the small group environment, their needs, hurts and disappointments surfaced. People cannot hide in the small group. God uses small group ministry to bring problems to the surface and ultimately bring healing.

The Holy Spirit's Desire for Edification

The Holy Spirit's ministry is to build up our lives, not tear them down. He is vitally interested in reconstructing people from the inside out. The word *edification*, in fact, literally means "to build or construct." Paul wrote to the Corinthian church:

> What then shall we say, brothers? When you come together, everyone has a hymn, or a word of instruction, a revelation, a tongue or an interpretation. All of these must be done for the strengthening [edifying] of the church.
>
> 1 Corinthians 14:26

Whether practicing the gifts of the Spirit in a large group or a small group, the goal is always the same: edification. I believe the small group is the best atmosphere for people's lives to be reconstructed and for them to grow in the grace and knowledge of Jesus Christ.

In the small group, the Holy Spirit, the Master Craftsman, challenges and changes people's lives. The intimate atmosphere of the small group makes it possible for this edification to take place. The smaller group allows each person to share, to minister and to receive ministry from one another. The Scriptures about love and caring come to life in this atmosphere, and ultimately bring healing to the lives of people.

Rebuilding the Inner World

It does not take long to notice that people outwardly suffer the symptoms of inner wounds. Proverbs 15:13

says, "A happy heart makes the face cheerful, but heart-ache crushes the spirit." The crushed spirit that characterizes so many is the result of childhood abuse, divorced parents, unforgiveness, resentment, the destructive habits of a parent, rejection, depression, guilt and various types of fear. There is such hurt, such buried anxiety and difficulty, in the lives of people both in and out of the Church.

People need a Savior to touch them and work healing in their hearts. Only God can heal and set people free, and that is why we need inner healing so much. Through inner healing, we can enter the grace that God has for us. People do not understand the buried hurt that is causing them to suffer so much. But God wants to touch them and set them free.

I remember one cell leader whom Celyce and I trained. She had come from an abusive background. As we began to train her, we saw God's healing start to take place, but we also noticed that her problems were far beyond the norm. She needed inner healing in order to function properly. In this case, we sent her for individual counseling as she continued in the training track. This was perfect for her, because she was able to grow in the grace and knowledge of Jesus Christ. She had not been able to function in everything God had for her because of all the emotional baggage that had pinned her down and would not allow her to continue in the truth. Her path stalled because these issues stalked her.

The situation in our world will surely get worse. It is estimated that six out of ten children born in the 1990s will live in single-parent households by the time they are eighteen years old.[1] Feelings of rejection among

American youth are now a normal way of life. Many find it extremely hard to forgive themselves for their parents' mistakes or their own past decisions. Past issues paralyze present activities and stymie future growth. The results include:

compulsive behavior
self-chastisement
doubt
feelings of unworthiness
denial of what God wants to give them

In the midst of this cultural meltdown, Christ is still head of the Church and Lord over all (see Matthew 28:18–20). God has a loving plan for every person, and He longs to heal the lonely, depressed and disenfranchised. Jesus wants not only to forgive people of their sins but also to heal them of their inner pain and emotional sickness. He offers peace in a world full of hurt and despair. An effective cell leader takes advantage of difficult moments to remind members that God is vitally concerned about every aspect of their lives and wants to provide inner healing.

The night that Michael came to my own small group, everything appeared normal. After the lesson on forgiveness from 1 Peter 4:8, however, his need for inner healing surfaced. He shared his deep resentment toward a pastor whom he felt had raped his daughter. Michael had been clinging to his bitterness toward this pastor, which left him joyless and enslaved. That night the Word of God reached deep into his soul, and Michael realized he needed to be set free from his bitterness, both for his own sake and in order to please Jesus Christ. During the prayer time, Michael confessed his bitterness, and the group members prayed for him to experience inner healing. God freed Michael that night from his bitterness and resentment, and he left the meeting filled with joy and peace.

Many people, like Michael, are afflicted from demonic attacks through bitterness or other sins. God wants to do great things, but we must allow Him to operate in our small groups to effect inner healing in group members.

The small, intimate atmosphere of the home is ideal for healing hurts caused by sin, the world and Satan. The leader should remind the cell members of verses like Isaiah 63:9: "In all their distress he too was distressed, and the angel of his presence saved them. In his love and mercy he redeemed them; he lifted them up and carried them all the days of old." King David's reminder of God's love is also good to use in the context of healing in the small group:

> My frame was not hidden from you when I was made in the secret place. When I was woven together in the depths of the earth, your eyes saw my unformed body. All the days ordained for me were written in your book before one of them came to be.
>
> Psalm 139:15–16

The small group leader can discern the need for inner healing by noticing erratic behavior among members, such as paralyzing fear and shyness, lack of trust, confusion, depression or compulsive behavior. At the appropriate time in the lesson, the leader might ask members to share difficult moments when they experienced pain and rejection in their own lives. The leader should encourage group members to share honestly and pray for one another to experience restoration, healing and a sense of community.

The good news is that Christ is the Healer. The Scriptures tell us that "He was despised and rejected by men, a man of sorrows, and familiar with suffering" (Isaiah 53:3). He is the only one who is able to understand all of the circumstances of our lives. The small group provides an excellent opportunity for people to share times of pain and grief and then receive the inner healing necessary to live a victorious Christian life.

Christ's called-out Church should be a hospital in this world. Many wounded people enter this hospital—people who have been beaten up by sin, Satan and all the atrocities that modern life throws at them. Jesus understands. The writer of Hebrews declared:

> Since the children have flesh and blood, he [Jesus] too shared in their humanity so that by his death he might destroy him who holds the power of death—that is, the devil. . . . Because he himself suffered when he was tempted, he is able to help those who are being tempted.
>
> Hebrews 2:14, 18

Group Healing

People need first to warm up to the small group before transformation can take place. Wise leaders encourage group members to share honestly and to pray for one another to experience restoration and healing.

Effective small group leaders get members involved so that each person begins to see him or herself as God's healing agent. Each member of Christ's body can minister healing to others. No one should sit on the sidelines.

When Monica arrived early to our cell group meeting, she began to pour out her heart: "I'm so thankful I'm no longer living with Andy. I feel clean inside, but it is still so hard; at times, I feel as though I need him." Frank and Kathy arrived in the middle of our conversation and began to minister to Monica from their own experience. My wife also spoke words of encouragement to her, and eventually all of us began to pray for Monica. My wife and Kathy understood Monica's needs more deeply than I, and their prayers hit the emotional nerve center of what Monica was going through.

Monica left that night a renewed person. She dedicated herself to live a pure, holy life—without her live-in boyfriend. Her healing came through the ministry of the Body of Christ. Notice the idea of group healing and group community. It is not about one person bringing about all the healing; it is about everyone ministering to one another. It is about getting our eyes off one person and onto everyone involved. Small group healing is not the preacher's job. Everyone participates, and through the entire group, God moves and blesses each one.

Miracles often occur when every member becomes a minister, and the members of the Church begin to see themselves as instruments of healing. In his book *Connecting*, author and psychologist Larry Crabb wrote:

> Ordinary people have the power to change other people's lives. . . . The power is found in connection, that profound meeting when the truest part of one soul meets the emptiest recesses in another. . . . When that happens, the giver is left more full than before and the receiver

less terrified, eventually eager, to experience even deeper, more mutual connection.[2]

The power of small group ministry is discovered by allowing each member to minister to and connect with each other. It is a time when confession, inner healing, transparent sharing and renewal happen. I love small group ministry because it allows the grace for everyone to be involved in the healing process. It opens the door for all people to take place in ministering to others and blessing others through powerful healing prayer.

Sensitivity to the Spirit

Sensitive small group leaders ask the Holy Spirit to manifest the needs of the members, knowing that the best agenda is the one that meets the needs of those present. When the leader has this in mind, he or she is willing to do what it takes to make that happen.

I attended one cell meeting in which the leader asked members to pick their favorite songs during the worship time. After each song, the cell leader asked the person to explain why he or she picked that particular song. One woman, Theresa, picked a song about renewal, and later began to sob. "I had an angry confrontation with my husband today. I discovered he's seeing another woman," she blurted out. "I feel so dirty. Please pray for me." The responsive, Spirit-led cell leader listened to Theresa without overloading her with Scripture and advice. Theresa felt God's love as the cell leader motioned for her to sit in a chair while the other members prayed for her. Theresa felt cleansed and healed as she left that prayer time. She had come to the meeting bruised and beaten down, but she left filled and encouraged.

The standard for success in small group ministry is whether or not the members leave the group edified—whether or not healing took place in people's lives—not whether a particular order or plan was followed.

Sensitivity is essential in small group ministry. Those who excel in small group ministry are those who are sensitive to needs. It is best to go into the cell group prayed up and open to whatever God has for the group. God will guide; He will lead. He will show the leader what is essential. We need to be sensitive to the needs of those who are present. God wants to work in our midst, but we must allow Him to work.

Silence That Promotes the Healing Process

When someone is facing a crisis, it is not the moment to say, "You just need to trust in the Lord. Don't you know that all things work together for good to those who love God, to those who are called according to His purpose?" This advice, while one hundred percent correct, will actually do more harm than good to a hurting, grieving person. Before becoming ready to hear advice, the person first must know that God's people will help bear the burden. He or she is longing for a listening ear—not a quick response of an often-quoted Scripture passage. Healing takes place in the silence of skilled listening and love. God is the sensitive Healer, and He desires that His people listen to others. Listening is so powerful; it works wonders because it causes people to feel special, loved and cared for. When someone shares a huge need,

73

we must allow God to flow in a special way and manifest Himself. Just be quiet. Be silent before God, and allow Jesus to minister to that person's needs.

After the burden is shared, there should be a moment of silent understanding. As group members empathize with the person, godly counsel will ensue: "Joan, I can relate to your fears and doubts brought on by your friend's cancer. When my brother faced brain cancer, I felt those same fears. I wrestled for days, wondering why God would allow this disease to strike my family. But then God showed me. . . ." The scales of past wounds will peel away, and the new creature in Christ will appear as the cell group ministers through empathetic listening.

It is this shared understanding that is so important: Not just one person is listening, but the entire group is involved. When a person is truly listened to, grace and love follow and bless everyone involved.

It is best for the cell leader to advise the group to listen, rather than quickly respond with pat answers. The cell leader must demonstrate, however, what she wants others to do by her own actions. People will not necessarily follow words, but they will follow actions. Preparing a healing community may take some time, but it is worth the wait. Healing through listening is God's powerful tool to heal a lost and hurting world.

Rebuilding through Encouragement

Listening opens the door for encouragement. Small group leaders bring healing by tuning their ears for the slightest reason to give praise. If there is even a hint of excellence, a great small group leader will spot it and acknowledge it. The enemy seeks to accuse each of us through lies that discourage. He might whisper to one group member, *No one respects you. You don't know the Bible well enough. You wouldn't dare make that comment.* The small group leader is God's agent to offer a word of encouragement that will bless the person abundantly and help him or her to speak up. Praise and encouragement are essential for healing to take place.

I remember being in one small group in which the leader offered a slight criticism to every response. "You almost have it," James would say. When another person responded to the answer, James retorted, "No, that's not it, but you're getting closer." The dance to find the right answer continued. *This is like a high school quiz,* I thought to myself. As James reached the last few questions, the participation ground to a screeching halt. No one wanted to risk embarrassment. The fear of failure permeated the room. A small group leader needs to listen intently, for healing actually comes in the listening process.

The best small group leaders view themselves as God's healing agents and encourage all to participate, knowing that encouragement is one of the primary ways to minister God's healing touch. They practice the words of Proverbs: "Pleasant words are a honeycomb, sweet to the soul and healing to the bones" (16:24). Great small group facilitators guard against any information or comments that are not edifying—that destroy rather than build up.

One member of my small group had a habit of mixing humor with sarcasm and half-truths. On one occasion I told the group to stretch out their hands to pray for a person, and that a few could gather around and lay hands on the person. This person said in a half-serious tone,

"The Bible doesn't tell us to stretch out our hands; it tells us to lay our hands on people." I did not know if he was joking or serious, but I did feel challenged, and I felt his comment was not edifying. The Holy Spirit told me to talk directly to him, sharing my concern. Because I have told the group repeatedly that gossip is a sin and that the Bible tells us to go directly to the offending person, I needed to model this truth. This person immediately received my words, apologized and communicated that he was only making a joke and meant nothing by the comment.

At times a small group leader will need to follow the words of Jesus and go privately to the person who has spoken unedifying words in the small group (see Matthew 18:15–17). If what was said affected the group negatively, ask the person to apologize to the entire group. This is one reason that I highly recommend that every small group leader have a coach: When difficult situations such as these arise, it is great to know there is an experienced leader with whom the small group leader can unload burdens and seek counsel.

Everyone who is attending a small group is in the process of growth and change as well. Because sinful human beings make up the membership of every small group, problems will inevitably occur, but often, careful instruction to the group about the Holy Spirit's desire to edify will set the standard and help avoid problems before they start.

Accountability and the Rebuilding Process

Even after healing takes place among group members, Satan will work overtime to discourage, condemn and entice people back into a web of lies and condemnation. Transparency without transformation is superficial.

Some people have become experts in unloading deep emotion without any desire or intention to change. In such cases, the healing never seeps down to change core values, but it only resides in the emotional realm. Great small group leaders revisit areas of confession to make sure transformation has taken place. Satan is a hard taskmaster. He never lets up. Because he hates us and wants to destroy us, he is always attacking and penetrating the darkness of our souls and minds. Group leaders need to follow up on what he has done in the lives of others. Only God can give the grace needed to reach empty hearts and minds. We need to be grace-givers, always allowing the Spirit of God to flow through us, ministering to people through the gifts of the Spirit and asking Jesus to take us, mold us and shape us.

When Vicki began attending a small group from the Verdugo Free Methodist Church in Los Angeles, California, in February 2002, her marriage was falling apart, and her drug problem masked hidden fears. Yet in the loving small group atmosphere, Vicki experienced healing and freedom from drugs. Her marriage was restored, and her husband, Tom, received Jesus Christ. Vicki grew in Christ as she shared struggles, received encouragement and applied God's Word to her situation.

As the months passed, Susan, the group leader, noticed that Vicki was once again taking large doses of medication and reverting to her old lifestyle. Susan had to confront Vicki with the fact that "when people are scared, they tend to turn to old coping mechanisms. But no matter what old coping mechanisms you turn to, you can't turn away from my love for you." Vicki began to cry, saying, "No matter how many times I've failed, you've never rejected me." Vicki testified that if it had not been for Susan and the group, she would have killed herself the year before.

Susan understood that healing was a process that needed constant follow-up. Great small group leaders realize that when a person (or a couple) reveals a struggle, he or she is reaching out for help, saying, "Pray for me" or "Help me." Victory occurs when true change becomes part of the person's lifestyle. The cell group should hold the person accountable to improve that behavior—not in a legislative, legalistic way, but through constant encouragement. There is a certain accountability that must take place, and Susan is a great example of that accountability. As a cell leader, you should hold those around you accountable to what they have experienced. Don't let them go unless they have been healed.

Not all healing will take place in the group environment. Sensitive leaders use the time before and after the meeting to inquire about transformation. A leader might say, for example, "Jim, you shared about your pornographic addiction and your need to break free from that habit. How are you doing in that area?" Even though Jim was touched through prayer, he needs follow-up and constant encouragement in order to remain free.

Some cell leaders insist on conducting small group meetings that are two to three hours long, but if this is the case, people will leave immediately afterward because of their busy schedules. I strongly recommend that a cell meeting end after one-and-a-half hours to allow time for refreshments and spontaneous interaction. It is often during the refreshment time that the best sharing, evangelism and community life take place.

Not all community or ministry happens in the cell group. Cells are often the springboard for one-on-one relationships that take place outside the meetings. Janet, a member of our cell group, silently suffered in her marriage because of a total blackout of communication. She wisely did not blurt out the hurt she carried (which would have maligned her husband to those in the group). She did, however, spend hours with my wife outside the cell meeting, receiving prayer and encouragement. God ministered to her in the small group environment but healed her in the relationships that extended from the cell.

Healing of the Spirit

The Church is a hospital—not a performing arts center. Jesus came, in fact, to heal the hurting and needy: He ate with the sinners and hung out with the disenfranchised. He was rejected by the religious rulers because He prioritized the needs of people over adherence to man-made laws.

After Jesus healed a blind man on the Sabbath, the Pharisees were convinced that He was not the Messiah because He had broken the Sabbath law. Jesus retorted, "For judgment I have come into this world, so that the blind will see and those who see will become blind" (John 9:39). The only ones Jesus could not heal were those who failed to grasp their own personal need for healing. Just like a doctor, He came to heal the sick, not the healthy.

Like Christ, the small group leader should gravitate toward those with needs in the group, offering Christ's healing power to the hurting. The leader must boldly proclaim Christ's desire to heal today—physically, spiritually and emotionally. The hospital nature of the cell group is a truism that we must accept: God's healing power is made manifest in the sweet atmosphere of the cell.

Leaders need Christlike humility and childlike faith as they minister God's healing power. When this takes place, members will catch on and begin praying for one another, seeing themselves as Christ's agents of healing. The full Gospel will be proclaimed, and all heaven will rejoice at the extension of Christ's bride, the Church.

Part 3

The
Spirit's Gifts
IN THE
SMALL GROUP

5

CHRIST'S BODY AND SMALL GROUPS

The amazing thing about Christ's Church is that He operates supernaturally through weak, sinful human beings. Our own humanity often gets in the way of what He wants to do, but Christ still calls us His Church.

The early first-century Christians faced the same battles and conflicts that we face today, and yet they were closer to the fire, to the birth of Christ's Church. Some believers in the New Testament Church were actually firsthand witnesses of Christ's death and resurrection. An even larger group experienced the outpouring of the Spirit on the Day of Pentecost.

The important questions are, What was church life like for these early believers? What encounters with the Spirit did they experience as they worshiped together?

One problem these early Christians avoided was any worry about buying land or constructing expensive buildings. Today, church programs, buildings and budgets easily cloud the true meaning of the Holy Spirit-driven church. The primitive Church was made up of nomadic, pilgrim people who met from house to house. For the most part, the Church did not build or own buildings on a large-scale basis until AD 323, although archeology has uncovered inscriptions of church buildings (other than house churches) as early as AD 150.[1]

The Intimate Nature of the Church

The Spirit-filled small group was the "normal" Church in the New Testament; it was never seen as an "addition" to the "real" Church. The small group *was* the Church. These smaller churches met together in larger groups for corporate celebrations whenever possible, but the small, Spirit-filled house churches were the main vehicle through which Christ's Body grew in the New Testament period.

In the small group atmosphere, believers experienced the nature of Christ's Church as a living, spiritual household of faith, a family, and the Holy Spirit energized the ministry of all believers through the gifts of the Spirit. Jesus raised up apostles, prophets, evangelists, pastors and teachers from among the lay believers to fine-tune the Church and further its growth (see Ephesians 4:9–16).

In the early chapters of Acts, we read that in addition to the home meetings, the believers met in the Temple (see Acts 2:46; 5:20, 25, 42) and in the portico of the Temple (see Acts 5:12). Persecution soon made large group gatherings difficult, and the preferred meeting place became the houses of the individual believers. These simple house churches became the primary type of the Church in the

New Testament period. The writers of Scripture commonly referred to the "*church* in the *house* of" an individual's name (see, for example, Acts 12:12; Romans 16:3–5; 1 Corinthians 16:19; Colossians 4:15; and Philemon 2).

Some have argued that the early Church would have chosen to meet in buildings had it not been for the persecution the believers experienced. The New Testament record, however, does not support this view. Even when the early Church had the liberty to meet openly in large group gatherings, the believers *chose additionally* to meet from house to house to pray together, administer the Lord's Supper and exercise the gifts of the Spirit (see Acts 2:46; 5:42).

The small group, therefore, highlighted early Church experience for the first three hundred years. The small group environment, in fact, is the one variable that held constant throughout the early Church period before Constantine legalized Christianity in the early part of the fourth century.

The Background of the New Testament

New Testament writers had the context of the house in mind when they composed their letters to various churches. Theologians remind us that the doctrine of the *inspiration of Scripture* refers to the moment the writer actually wrote the Scripture passage. The authors' audiences and contexts, therefore, are imperative information if we are to apply a particular passage of Scripture to the 21st century.

When the New Testament writers wrote their letters, they were writing to house churches. When they wrote about the Body of Christ, the family of God and the temple of the Holy Spirit, they were envisioning the intimate home fellowships where the believers actually experienced such images. John Mallison, small group writer and teacher, reflects on the early Church context, saying, "It is almost certain that every mention of a local church or meeting, whether for worship or fellowship, is in actual fact a reference to a church meeting in a house."[2] Our tendency is to commit the error of projecting our own experience upon the New Testament writers, rather than the other way around. Thus, when we project our present-day church-building experience, for example, back onto the context of Scripture, we fail to understand Scripture properly.

Christ's Own Body

The biblical theme of giftedness and Body life is exciting. In all three passages in which Paul wrote about the Body of Christ (see Romans 12; 1 Corinthians 12–14; Ephesians 4), he defined each part according to giftedness. The only way to know where a person fits in the Body of Christ is to discover his or her giftedness. The home atmosphere of the early Church gave each person ample opportunity to test, prove and discover his or her own spiritual giftedness.

Paul described the Church as Christ's own Body, made up of distinct parts (see 1 Corinthians 12:27). Christ supernaturally energizes each member through the Holy Spirit and places each one in His Body according to the distinct spiritual gifts each one possesses (see 1 Corinthians 1:18; 2:9–10). Christ distributes His gifts on an equal basis regardless of race, nationality, socio-economic status or gender. The diverse parts come together to form one Body (see 1 Corinthians 12:12–26). Unity reigns because the

Spirit sets each person in the Body according to His will (see 1 Corinthians 12:11).

Today, more than ever, we need to get back to the small group as the primary place to exercise spiritual gifts. It is the most natural context for worship and prayer together. It is the best place to find encouragement and accountability as we grow in our relationship with Christ. It is also the most spontaneous and biblical place for the discovery of our spiritual gifts.

Spiritual gifts are given for the good of the Church. Small groups are wonderful places to experiment with our "unknown" spiritual gifts, even risking failure, because we know that the small group will be forgiving of our mistakes. Everyone has a job to do in the small group. Everyone is noticed in the small group. Thus, we notice the spiritual gifts in which others operate well and the jobs they enjoy doing.

Some people have tried to mobilize the gift ministry apart from a small group setting, but I believe it is far more fruitful to promote spiritual gifts through the small group ministry. In small groups, encouragement and accountability are more likely to occur spontaneously. In the small group setting, the Holy Spirit is more likely to be working through relationships to build a quality of spiritual life and unity among the members. This environment seems to be a natural place to use the gifts of the Spirit for the common good.

In the early Church, those members who successfully exercised their gifts in the home-church context were lifted up to the greater responsibility of exercising their gifts in a broader home-church network, or perhaps even in the celebration gathering (see Acts 2:46). In Acts 6, when the apostles told the people to look for leaders among them, they seemed to already know who the gifted ones were (see verses 5–6).

When the early Church read the letters addressed to them by Paul and Peter concerning the spiritual gifts, they knew immediately what to do with the information. They did not need to take a spiritual-gift test or call a spiritual-gift counselor. No, they simply exercised their gifts in the context of the relationships they had established in their home-church community.

The Spirit-filled small group is a place in which the Body of Christ comes alive through the supernatural working of each part. The atmosphere is alive with possibility and order, since the Spirit is the one directing what takes place. The best leadership stays in tune with the Spirit's still, small voice, allows God's peace to reign and promotes edification in all things. Through the gifts, the parts of the Body are distinguished and the Church expresses Christ's purposes completely. Small groups are where spiritual gifts are unwrapped, and individuals get the chance to minister through the power of the Holy Spirit.

The Family of God

I am grateful I have a dad, a mom, two brothers and one sister. We share a common genetic bloodline and heritage. I was born into the Comiskey household on May 6, 1956, but one day in September 1973, I experienced a new birth into a different household, the family of God. In Ephesians 3:14–15, Paul wrote: "For this reason I kneel before the Father, from whom his whole family in heaven and on earth derives its name." God is our heavenly Father, and we are God's chosen people, adopted into His family, the Church.

I was birthed into this new family, which includes all believers throughout eternity and all Christians worldwide, but also those believers with whom I am personally in relationship in my local church. The home group in my local church highlights this truth experientially. Those in our small group in Moreno Valley, California, are part of my spiritual family. Dave celebrates birthdays with my daughters. My kids spend the night at Sunitha's house. Brock brings crafts for my kids to play with. All of them come over on New Year's Day and for other special events. We are family. Dave, Sunitha and Brock are all single, and so they naturally and supernaturally bonded with my own family both in and outside of the small group. Yet we also relate as Christ's family to the other families in our church.

The Porters, for example, joined our small group in 2004. Their lives changed as they experienced the family atmosphere and the love among the members. Their twelve–year-old daughter, Bethany, found a true spiritual family. She wrote the following poem and read it to our group on New Year's Eve to express her appreciation:

> Even though the years go by one at a time,
> Even though the memories are gone,
> Good ones, sad ones, fun ones, bad ones,
> We'll always remember the good times
> We had laughing and playing, eating and talking.
> Being together is the best thing ever.
> You're my family, and I'm your family.
> We're a family in Christ.
> Together we'll tell the people
> How much Jesus loves them and cares for them.
> Though this year is gone
> I want to tell you how much fun I had

Serving Jesus with you.
So this is the end of the poem.
Hope you enjoyed it.
I just want you to know I'll always love you
And care for you.

The Porters are part of our family. We have the same parents (the Trinity). We have been adopted into God's heavenly family, and therefore we can honestly call each other "brothers and sisters." There is nothing quite like the atmosphere of a home to confirm the fact that we are indeed God's family.

The Tendency toward Institutionalism

Many North American churches promote the gifts of the Spirit in the context of ministries within the Church. Often the list of spiritual gifts found in Romans, 1 Corinthians and Ephesians are correlated with organizational roles. If someone has the gift of teaching, for example, that person would be recommended to teach Sunday school. The person with the gift of helps would serve on the building committee, count offerings or fold bulletins. Those with the gift of mercy might join the women's missionary circle. The progression usually proceeds like this:

- A church develops a wide variety of programs and ministries.
- Spiritual-gift tests are offered to the members to help them decide where they can exercise their gifts among the ministries and programs that have been created.

- The members are placed within one of the programs and ministries that the church has to offer.

The main problems with this approach are that it is top heavy, it is impersonal and it promotes the program-based church. Attempts at institutionalizing gifts are well intentioned, but they miss a vital and central reality: Gifts are not primarily related to institutional maintenance. Gifts are related to the building up of persons and are best exercised in direct person-to-person contact.

People do not use the gifts of the Holy Spirit to further the enterprise of building the Church. The Holy Spirit, rather, occupies people and uses those people according to His will, His timing and the situation. Too often we become preoccupied with the workings of the gifts of the Spirit and trying to discover exactly what our own spiritual gifts are. Yet in reality, the gifts are not *ours*—they are *His*, and He manifests those gifts as He pleases.

The Priesthood of All Believers

Ministry is not meant to be practiced by a few elite people. Revelation 1:6 declares that Christ has called the Church to be a kingdom of priests. Those who are specifically gifted to hold offices in the Church (apostles, prophets, evangelists, pastors and teachers) are in the unique position of equipping Christ's Church to function as priests and ministers (see Ephesians 4:10–12).

As children of the Reformation, most Protestant Christians today would agree that every believer is called to be a minister. From a practical perspective, however, most people sit back and watch the paid clergy do the work. Often the church settles for the priesthood of all *educated* believers—only "gifted" or "highly educated" people use their gifts in any significant way. Elton Trueblood once said:

> All of us suffer from a terrible sickness in our churches. It is called *Spectatoritis*. We speak of the congregation as the audience. We are not the audience; we are the actors. . . . If we sincerely believe the Gospel, we have to believe that God has a vocation for each of us. The secret is participation, participation, participation.[3]

The spectator nature of the Church does not turn members into ministers or make disciples of the multitudes. It fails to promote the priesthood of all believers, and it overemphasizes the *hearing* of the Word. Although we must always rejoice in those whom God has called to preach, the Scriptures tell us that we are all ministers and that God Himself has "made us to be a kingdom and priests to serve his God and Father" (Revelation 1:6).

Most seminaries teach potential pastors how to preach, counsel, visit, conduct funerals and weddings, administer the sacraments and otherwise fulfill the needs of the church. Seminary teaching is based on the view that the church is the place where people gather to hear the preacher speak. Preaching and teaching gifts are highlighted, but other gifts such as prophecy, healing, service, administration, mercy and words of knowledge have little visibility. The result is strong teaching, but little life in the Body. A few people are busy, powerful—and tired.

Korean Pastor David Yonggi Cho made a revolutionary discovery in the early 1970s. At that time he was bone-weary from trying to pastor his growing church—he almost died of exhaustion in the process. Out of necessity, he began training his lay people to minister to one another in small groups.

Now, 25,000 groups later, Cho has the largest church in the history of Christianity, and he has birthed the modern-day cell-church movement. Cho writes:

> In our cell groups, although the leader teaches from the Word of God, based on the church-approved outline, the other members have the opportunity to bring a word of prophecy, tongues and interpretation, a word of knowledge or a word of wisdom. Each can pray for the sick and in faith believe God will hear his prayer and heal that person.[4]

The home-cell atmosphere enhances the ministry of all believers who are using their spiritual gifts.

Cho allows the leaders and members to use their gifts in the small group. The great benefit of doing so in this context is that it takes some of the ministry out of the hands of a "chosen few" and places it in the hands of the laity. No one is allowed to sit passively. Everyone must be involved. Due to the multiplication of the groups, there is a constant need for new leaders, interns, hostesses, song leaders and evangelistic teams. The responsibility is shared among many people, and in the intimacy of a small, closely knit group, Christians can exercise their spiritual gifts.

The challenge for those leading the small groups is to uncover the gifts of each member, helping each person to become a priest and minister. In Romans 15:14, Paul declared: "I myself am convinced, my brothers, that you yourselves are full of goodness, complete in knowledge and competent to instruct one another." Paul believed the Holy Spirit was competent and able to work among the churches he established. And yet Paul also realized that the only way people were going to feel competent to minister was if they were given the opportunity to minister. Small group leaders have the incredible challenge of giving others the opportunity to serve and eventually lead a group.

When believers are called out, encouraged and given meaningful opportunities to serve, many will act on that inner motivation and preparation of the Holy Spirit. Everyone has a face, a name, a life. In this context of belonging, the spiritual gifts are able to flow freely. In a loving environment, group members are willing to risk and use the gifts they have.

The discovery of the spiritual gifts of a small group's members is not just for the individual's benefit—or even the small group's benefit. The hope is that those who discover their gifts through the small group will also become involved in the larger context of the church. Many may benefit as gifts are discovered and exercised.

At Wellspring, the church where I minister, we prepare lessons based on the sermons and give them to the small group leaders. We give them liberty, however, to cover other topics as the Spirit leads. We encourage the groups to exercise their spiritual gifts and to practice the priesthood of all believers.

The postmodern culture emphasizes equal access and participation. While the modern world could be described as the *age of representation*, the postmodern world is the *age of participation*. We live in an age of karaoke. Everyone wants to be involved. Everyone can stand up and sing a song. Bill Easum, author and consultant, speaking of today's emerging church, said: "The priesthood of the believer will finally emerge. Most of the ministry in healthy churches will be done by the laity. Lay pastors will be the norm."[5]

The Size of the Group

In the early Church, if a household fellowship grew too large, the leaders of established household churches would call out a new leader and begin a new house church. New leadership matured in the gift-rich environment of the house church. The church flourished within organic home fellowships.

My own small group eventually stagnated because we had too many people attending. No one dared invite a new person into our fellowship because our living room was already packed with adults and kids. We all enjoyed great fellowship, excellent worship and the Holy Spirit's presence, and we were fed from the Word during each meeting. But we also began to notice that no one talked about evangelism. Inwardly, everyone was thinking, *Where would we put the new people?*

My wife and I wrestled with this "blessed dilemma" of having too many people. We knew inwardly who would make ideal multiplication leaders—a couple who brought all five of their children to the small group each week. But when we approached them about it, they replied, "We're not ready yet." We prayed and continued to wrestle with God over this issue.

One night after our prayer meeting, the husband approached me about the lack of evangelism in the group. I was able to explain our problem of group size. The Spirit spoke to him that he and his family needed to open a group. This couple is now leading a group, and intimacy and outreach can now be maintained in both groups.

Some people feel that the original small group must stay together forever, but the concept of the gifts of the Spirit should actually propel the group to reach out and raise up new leaders. If a group grows too large, not everyone will be able to use his gifts, and so it is imperative that new groups grow and multiply. When people in a small fellowship discover and use their spiritual gifts, the multiplication of ministry is more effective and vital.

A small group ministry that focuses on multiplication will be more successful when each group believes in mobilizing its members' gifts. Exercising spiritual gifts keeps a group healthy, and healthy cells multiply. The quality of caring within the group will draw others, including unbelievers.

Someone once said, "Community begins at three and ends at fifteen." Keeping the group small maintains the feeling of community. Only in the intimacy of a small, closely knit group will people confess their faults one to another in order to be healed (see James 5:16). Open sharing becomes difficult when the group grows to more than fifteen. The quest for community and the desire for everyone to exercise spiritual gifts should stir each small group to develop new leaders in order to eventually multiply new groups. This will offer fresh hope to people in need.

Some people are effective at reaching out, while others are more adept at nourishing new and older believers. Members with the gifts of evangelism and exhortation are great at bringing others into the group. Once there, members with a hospitality gift make newcomers feel welcome, and those with pastoring and mercy gifts offer consistent, quality care.

Many facilitators act as if small group evangelism is primarily their own responsibility. They take the burden on themselves to grow the group, rather than depending on the giftedness of everyone involved. Small group evangelism, however, is more like fishing with a net than a pole. The group aspect of cell evangelism takes the burden off the leader and places it on everyone in the cell. Pole fishing is done individually, while net fishing requires the help of many hands. Net fishing is a group effort, and it results in catching more fish; fishing with a pole catches only one fish at a time. When Jesus said to Simon and Andrew, "Come, follow me . . . and I will make you fishers of men," He was talking about becoming net fishermen—that is the way they fished back then. The beauty of cell evangelism today is the casting out and drawing in of the net as a result of the group effort (see Mark 1:16–17).

Bill Mangham's small group often planned outreach events. On one such occasion, he used the story of Zacchaeus, the tax collector whom Jesus transformed (see Luke 19:1–10), for their lesson. Everyone helped plan the meeting: One person brought refreshments; another prepared the icebreaker; Bill's wife, Ann, took care of the house; and everyone in the group prayed over the list of invitees (family, friends and work associates) and then actively invited those whom Jesus brought to mind. Four non-Christians attended the group for the first time that night. The group reached out to the newcomers and made them feel like family.

After the lesson, Bill invited everyone to meet Jesus in the quietness of his or her own heart. No one knew if anyone had accepted Jesus until the refreshment time afterward. Rene, one member of the group, asked the couple he had invited what they thought about the lesson. They told him that they had accepted Jesus during the prayer time. Jesus transformed this couple. They became faithful members of the small group and started attending the larger gathering celebration services as well.

What happened in Bill Mangham's cell group is not unique, yet most evangelistic training in the United States concentrates on the individual. Individuals receive instruction on how to share the Gospel at work, at home or in school. In contrast, small group evangelism is a shared experience. Everyone gets involved—from the person who invites the guests, to the one who provides refreshments, to the one who leads the discussion. The team plans, comes up with evangelism strategies and finds new contacts together. Small groups provide a great atmosphere for non-Christians.

A Large-Group Context for Spiritual Gifts

As I have researched small groups in various churches and contexts around the world, I have noticed that not all small group-based churches emphasize spiritual giftedness to the same degree. Some prefer that individual members exercise many of the gifts in the context of a larger group gathering. These gifts might include prophetic utterances and other such manifestations, including tongues and interpretation. The reason for wanting these gifts to be manifested in a larger group setting is the desire that pastors and elders be present when such gifts are exercised.[6]

While I respect and understand the reasons why some small group-based churches choose to operate this way, I am concerned that far fewer members will actually be able to exercise their gifts because of these limitations. Very few members, for example, are bold enough to grab a microphone when there are thousands of people present and calmly give a prophecy, a word in tongues or an interpretation.

I speak these words from personal experience. I remember back in 1975, sitting in the big crowd at Melodyland Christian Center in Anaheim, California, where Pastor Ralph Wilkerson formerly pastored. I would wait in the audience with my newly discovered gift of prophecy. About a thousand people were present in the service. After worship, Pastor Wilkerson would provide time for people to exercise their spiritual gifts. I waited for the right time, and then with my emotions high and my knees trembling, I stood up and let loose with a prophecy loud enough for as many people as possible to hear. Was it natural for me to do that? No way. But in all honesty, it was one of the only opportunities I was given to exercise the gift I believed God had given me. I had not yet started my home group at that time, and I wanted to be obedient to use what God had given me.

While a prophetic outburst from this zealous young Christian back in 1975 might have been admirable, it was not reproducible. God gave me the grace to do it, but most people, particularly the shy or timid, would find it difficult to experience, test or even discover their spiritual gifts in such a setting.

In a smaller group, however, people *can* learn to exercise their gifts without fear or intimidation. My growing conviction, in fact, is that the large group context is the *least* effective place to learn to exercise spiritual gifts. Only a few believers can actually exercise their gifts in a large group atmosphere. How many can lead worship? How many can preach? How many can usher? In reality, opportunities to exercise the gifts in such a setting are limited.

Granted, both small groups and large groups can provide believers with the opportunity to exercise their spiritual giftedness. I do know that we need to discern what God wants. He is the one who guides and directs, and He wants us to use our gifts in both larger worship settings of celebration and in our cell groups. But I believe the correct order should place a higher priority on the small group than on the large group. People can learn to exercise their spiritual gifts in the small group, and then as they build their confidence, they can find ways to use their gifts in the larger worship context.

In the small group, a person can test, fail, grow, test again and continue to learn. Debby, for example, has the talent of playing the guitar, which is empowered by her gifts of leadership and prophecy. She faithfully plays her guitar during the Wednesday night cell meetings. Eventually, those in leadership noticed her faithfulness and abilities and asked her to join the worship team on Saturday night. Gifts are often discovered in the small group that can aid the rest of the church.

Both small group and large group contexts are important in discovering the gifts of the Spirit. The normal order should be to use one's gifts faithfully in the small group context first and then graduate to both small and large group settings.

The early Church demonstrated how Spirit-filled groups excel in using the gifts, representing Christ's Body on earth and releasing everyone to become priests and ministers of the living God. As we follow in their footsteps, the entire Church will be built up and drawn closer to God, the Giver of the gifts.

6

HOW THE GIFTS WORK
IN SMALL GROUPS

I have noticed a deadly disease that plagues many small group leaders. It is called the "Super Leader Syndrome." It is deadly because it often leads to the small group leader's dropping out of sight or resigning. This disease might allow the leader to survive for several months or even several years, but my observation is that it is almost always terminal.

The small group leader is the facilitator—not the workhorse. He or she is the person who orchestrates the work that the whole group, in turn, carries out. And this is where the gifts of the Spirit play such a vital role.

There is simply too much work for one leader to do alone. Consider the following pressures that a cell leader places upon himself when he embraces the statement, "I need to do all the work": He must prepare and facilitate all the various parts of the weekly meetings, ultimately making it look polished and professional; he must personally reach his lost friends (and his members' lost friends) for Christ; he must meet with everyone in the group as often as possible to mentor and disciple them into strong believers; he must train interns or apprentices by having them watch what he does, so that when they get their own group, they will know what to do.

Instead of doing everything yourself—which will never create a feeling of community or equip new leaders—involve the entire team through the gifting of each person! Ask others to help you in every aspect of cell life and leadership:

- Discover what others like to do according to their giftings.
- Delegate all the various parts of your weekly meetings to others, a month at a time, and watch them learn as they do it. For example, ask someone in the group to be in charge of refreshments, someone else to be in charge of prayer, worship, the ministry time, etc.
- Ask others to host.
- Establish mentor relationships among the small group members.
- Develop a team that will help you make plans.

All of this can be accomplished through members' understanding of the place of their spiritual gifts and having a one hundred-percent commitment to allow others to use their gifts and talents. By involving others, your group will become an exciting place of ministry and growth, and you will not feel like Atlas, with the weight of the world on your shoulders.

In reality, many believers are bored with their Christian lives, especially if all they seem to do is go to church, sit and listen to sermons and then come home again. Spiritual gifts allow people to discover their place in the Body and to serve with others while following Jesus. In a small group atmosphere, believers work together to edify the Body and reach out to those without Christ. Spiritual gifts, exercised in love, help each person discover his or her purpose in relationship to the Church.

The Definition of Spiritual Gifts

In the Greek language, the original language of the New Testament, the word *charismata* means "gift." *Charismata* refers to "something bestowed out of grace, favor or special kindness." In fact, the Greek word *charis*, the first half of the word *charismata*, means "grace." The gifts of the Holy Spirit, then, are God's undeserving grace endowments to born-again believers. The gifts of the Spirit are simply the extension of God's grace to His people.

The connection between grace and gifts is clearly seen in Romans 12:6, where Paul wrote, "We have different gifts [*charismata*], according to the grace [*charis*] given us." Some people are fond of referring to the gifts of the Spirit as gracelets because of the intimate connection that spiritual gifts have with God's grace.[1]

The Holy Spirit's Sovereign Role

The Holy Spirit owns the gifts: They are gifts *of* the Spirit. The Spirit might lend one, two or more of these gifts to believers, but the believer must always realize that the Holy Spirit owns them and is the only one who can make them work successfully.

The sovereign Spirit distributes His gifts according to His plan and purpose. Paul wrote in 1 Corinthians 12:7 and 11:

> Now to each one the manifestation of the Spirit is given for the common good. . . . All these are the work of one and the same Spirit, and he gives them to each one, just as he determines.

The Holy Spirit equips the Church with spiritual gifts in order that it may serve Christ, because the Church is the Bride of Christ. As the supreme Head of the Church, Christ guides and directs believers through the work of the Holy Spirit.

One of the key uses of the gifts is to give clarity and purpose. Leaders lead. Administrators administrate. Prophets guide. Apostles pave new trails. God uses the gifts of knowledge, wisdom and prophecy to encourage and edify. The gifts of helps, mercy and hospitality remind us of God's care and love. Teachers keep us on the right path. Those with the gift of discernment protect us from demonic forces. As the *gracelets* of God's Spirit move among His people, the Church of Jesus Christ functions correctly.

The Believer's Role in Gift Use

The believer is called to discover which gifts the Holy Spirit has already given to him or her as an individual. We do not choose which gifts we receive, but we must develop the ones we have been given for we will be held accountable. Peter began his exhortation on the gifts by saying, "The end of all things is near" (1 Peter 4:7). He concluded the passage by saying:

> Each one should use whatever gift he has received to serve others, faithfully administering God's grace in its various forms. If anyone speaks, he should do it as one speaking the very words of God. If anyone serves, he should do it with the strength God provides, so that in all things God may be praised through Jesus Christ. To him be the glory and the power for ever and ever.
>
> 1 Peter 4:10–11

In the light of Christ's coming, Peter reminds us that we must develop and use our gifts, whether the gift lies in the category of speaking (teaching, prophecy or exhortation) or serving (helps, mercy or giving). In Matthew 25:14–30, Jesus told the parable of the talents; we are accountable for the gifts and talents given to us.

Scripture exhorts the believer to desire spiritual gifts (1 Corinthians 14:1). Paul even implied that it was acceptable to desire certain gifts above others (such as prophecy over tongues). The issue of desire flows into the idea of expectancy. Not only should the believer desire spiritual gifts, but he should also expect God to make those gifts manifest. Because it is clear from Scripture that the Holy Spirit wants this to take place in His Church, the next step is to expect Him to do so.

I once talked to a group of pastors about spiritual gifts. Some were actively practicing all of the spiritual gifts, while others were cautious due to past experiences. Despite their differences, however, the one thing everyone agreed upon was the need to *expect* God to work. Active participation in the spiritual gifts creates expectancy that God is working. Unfortunately, expectancy is a missing piece in many small groups and churches. Weary leaders long ago gave up expecting God to work. Practicing the spiritual gifts renews the passion of the people to see God working in the group. Some small group leaders over-organize the agenda, to the point that at times it appears the Holy Spirit must make a prior appointment in order to be involved! Regimented organization can stifle the Holy Spirit's move in a group. Effective small group leaders leave room for the Holy Spirit to break in and manifest Himself through the giftings of His people.

Along with the instruction to develop, desire and expect the gifts, Scripture tells us not to "put out the Spirit's fire," and immediately afterward it instructs us, "Do not treat prophecies with contempt" (1 Thessalonians 5:19–20). If we agree that Paul's words are applicable for believers living in the 21st century, we must allow and expect and practice the flow of *charismata*. Some people resist gift involvement because of:

fear of fanaticism

fear of failure

fear that use of the gifts will mean an increased commitment to Jesus Christ

fear of disorder

While a legitimate concern for disorder or false prophecy may exist, the scriptural mandate is that we allow the Spirit to move freely among us.

A final principle with regard to the gifts is to exercise love in all things. Paul conveniently sandwiched the "love chapter" (1 Corinthians 13) directly between chapters on spiritual gifts (1 Corinthians 12 and 14).

Paul was reminding the Church that spiritual gifts must have the grand objective of edification, rather than showmanship or sensationalism. The Spirit energizes people to use the gifts with the goal of serving others and ultimately blessing the Body of Christ.

Because spiritual gifts are not for our own benefit but to bless others, love must guide the process. If a spiritual gift does not edify someone else, it is best not to use it. The Holy Spirit's love also helps those who are exercising gifts in teams to walk in unity. Because no one Christian has all of the spiritual gifts, we need each other in the exercise of those spiritual gifts.

Love is pure and longsuffering. If we pray for someone to be healed, for example, and that person does not appreciate the effort, it is easy to become defensive and even angry. This applies to any of the gifts. Perhaps Sarah has the gift of helps and offers to clean Sandra's house during Sandra's last months of pregnancy. But perhaps Sandra does not even say thanks for the effort. This would upset anyone in the "natural" sense, but Sarah helped because she felt led to do so—she was exercising her gift out of a pure heart and is not offended.

Natural Talents and Gifts

The *charismata* are not the same as natural talents or skills. Spiritual gifts are manifestations of the Holy Spirit through a believer in a given situation. Spiritual gifts are given only to believers, but after conversion, every believer receives a spiritual gift.

Natural talents are aptitudes and abilities found in both believers and nonbelievers. Albert Einstein had a natural intellectual ability, enabling him to decipher complex mathematical equations. Yet because he was not a believer, Einstein did not possess a spiritual gift.

Apart from the spiritual distinction, there is often an overlap between the gifts of the Spirit and natural talents. A person with the gift of teaching, for example, will most likely be articulate in teaching outside of the Church. Most of the time, believers do not change into totally different people when exercising their gifts. Christians who use their natural talents in God's service should ask God to use and bless what they are doing with that talent. Christians who are manifesting a spiritual gift make themselves open to a move of the Spirit whenever and wherever He so wills.

The Fruit of the Spirit and Gifts

The fruit of the Spirit comes from the Spirit Himself. Because the Spirit dwells in every believer, so does the fruit of the Spirit. As the name implies, the fruit of the Spirit is part of the character of the Spirit that is made manifest in the believer's life.

The gifts, in contrast, represent specific activities of the Spirit of God—not His character. The gifts of the Spirit are manifestations of the Spirit given in order to edify the Body of Christ and cause it to function better.

Anyone operating in the gifts of the Spirit should do so with the fruit present. It is possible for a believer to exercise the gifts of the Spirit without showing the fruit of the Spirit; this is unfortunate, but entirely possible.

The Number of Gifts

The gifts are listed in three major biblical passages: Ephesians 4, Romans 12 and 1 Corinthians 12–14. Paul mentioned some gifts in all three passages and others in only certain passages. The fact that he pointed out different gifts in relation to different churches during different time periods has caused many people—myself included—to conclude that Paul was simply identifying particular gifts at work, not declaring that only certain gifts existed. The following chart, representing four "lists" or groupings that Paul gave in the three major passages, helps us understand his placement of gifts.

Ephesians 4:11	Romans 12:6-8	1 Corinthians 12:7-10	1 Corinthians 12:28-30
Apostles Prophets Evangelists Pastors	Prophecy	Prophecy	Apostles Prophets
Teachers	Teaching Service Exhortation Giving Ruling Mercy		Teachers
		Word of wisdom Word of knowledge Faith Healing Miracles Discerning of spirits	Healings Miracles
			Helps Administrators
		Tongues Interpretation of tongues	Tongues Interpretation of tongues

I do not believe that Paul's intention was to give the Church a close-ended view of the gifts of the Spirit. I take the approach that additional gifts are available for believers today. In other words, I do not believe that the gifts are limited only to the ones listed in these three passages.

Writers on the gifts of the Spirit have differing opinions on the number of spiritual gifts represented in the Bible. Here are a few examples: Ray Stedman suggests there are 16 or 17 gifts. C. Peter Wagner believes there are 27. Robert J. Clinton lists 18 gifts. Rick Yohn lists 20. John Wimber describes 28.[2] The number of gifts a person comes up with really depends on how that person defines *charismata* and the breadth of his interpretation. My point is that we should allow for flexibility when defining the spiritual gifts and remain open for the Holy Spirit to reveal additional gifts.

The Categories of Gifts

In the next chapter, I will define specific gifts more fully. But for our purposes in this chapter, here is a list of the gifts, in categories, that seem to make the most sense.[3]

The service gifts include:

Administration (1 Corinthians 12:28)
Helps (1 Corinthians 12:28)
Giving (Romans 12:8)
Mercy (Romans 12:8)

Service (Romans 12:7)
Faith (1 Corinthians 12:9)

The equipping gifts include:

Exhortation (Romans 12:8)
Wisdom (1 Corinthians 12:8)
Knowledge (1 Corinthians 12:8)
Teaching (1 Corinthians 12:28)
Pastoring (Ephesians 4:11)
Apostleship (1 Corinthians 12:28)
Evangelism (Ephesians 4:11)
Leadership (Romans 12:8)

The prayer and worship gifts include:

Prophecy (1 Corinthians 12:10)
Tongues (1 Corinthians 12:10)
Interpretation of tongues (1 Corinthians 12:10)
Healing (1 Corinthians 12:9)
Miracles (1 Corinthians 12:10)
Discernment of spirits (1 Corinthians 12:10)

Some *additional* gifts that are sometimes included in lists such as this one include: celibacy, voluntary poverty, hospitality, missions, exorcism, martyrdom, craftsmanship, artistic creativity and music. I will not be defining these *additional* gifts in this book, although various resources do explain them.[4] The only gift that is not specifically listed in Scripture that I will cover in this book is the gift of prayer, which I will cover in the last chapter.

Gifts of Successful Small Group Leaders

One key question to ask is whether or not it is necessary for a small group leader to possess a particular gift. The quest to discover the answer to that question was one of the factors that motivated me to administer surveys to seven hundred small group leaders in eight different countries. One of the questions on the survey concerned the leader's spiritual gifting. The leaders in the study were asked to write down what they believed their specific spiritual gift was. My theory before conducting the research was that specific gifts, such as evangelism and leadership, would correlate with a leader's effectiveness in growing and multiplying a group.

Surprisingly, the results of the statistical study showed no such correlation. Instead, the survey showed that those leaders with the gift of mercy were just as effective in growing and multiplying a small group as those who had the gift of evangelism.

I believe the reason for this finding is that successful cell leaders do not depend solely on their own gifts: They rely on the Holy Spirit's power to marshal the gifts of everyone in the small group. Great cell leaders truly see themselves as facilitators of others. They do not try to do everything themselves. They do not wear the "Super Leader" shirt. The best small group leaders, in fact, get out of the way and allow energized small group members to lead the way.

I have arrived at the conclusion that successful facilitation of a small group is related more to the spiritual maturing process of a believer than to the gifting that a leader possesses. Nothing matures a believer more than depending on God to prepare a lesson, facilitate the small group, care for the members and motivate the group to reach nonbelievers. The Holy Spirit uses the process of small group facilitation to grow and mature the leader, and I am convinced that anyone can successfully facilitate a small group, although not everyone will do so.[5]

The Reception of the Gifts

There are two views about the reception of the gifts of the Spirit: the constitutional view and the situational view.

The Constitutional View

The constitutional view holds that the gifts reside in the believer as a semi-permanent endowment. Most writers on the gifts of the Spirit, including C. Peter Wagner, take the constitutional view, believing that once we receive the gifts of the Holy Spirit, we receive those gifts for life. This is the basic teaching:

Each Christian has already received the gift(s) for life,
We must discover and use our gift(s), and
We must be content with the gift(s) we have been given.

Most tests to determine spiritual gifts are based on this model. A believer simply fills out a questionnaire that will, in turn, determine his or her spiritual gifting.

The problem with this model is that it assumes the Holy Spirit will only use a believer within his or her areas of gifting. This is why some pastors do not emphasize the gifts of the Spirit in their churches: They have found it to be counterproductive in developing mature disciples. While hoping to encourage involvement in diverse Christian ministry, for instance, these pastors find that believers want to grow only in the one or two areas determined by their spiritual gifting profiles. Taking this view to its extreme, some believers refuse to minister outside their "identified" gifts.

Reflecting on the discovery and use of spiritual gifts, Richard Gaffin, professor at Westminster Theological Seminary, comments on the problem of the constitutional view:

> One way not to proceed is to take the "spiritual inventory" approach and ask: What is it that I would like for my spiritual specialty? What is "my thing" spiritually that sets me apart from other believers? The New Testament would have us take a more functional, or situational, approach to identifying spiritual gifts. The key question to ask is this: What needs are there in the situation where God has placed me?[6]

The Situational View

The situational view suggests that the gifts reside with the Church and that the Holy Spirit endows believers with particular gifts as the need arises. In the situational view, any member of Christ's Church can operate in each and every gift, if the Spirit so wills it.

The late John Wimber said, "I believe and teach that the believer can move in all spiritual gifts in accordance with God's timing and purpose. Previously we have limited ourselves to one or more of the gifts and have shied away from the rest."[7] Wimber defined spiritual gifts as "supernatural manifestations of the Spirit of God, given momentarily so that God's love, charity, kindness and grace may be shed abroad among His people."[8]

In the situational view of ministry, the work of the Holy Spirit can be carried out in any environment, because the Holy Spirit may choose to drop new *gracelets* on His Church at any time, depending on the need and situation. Paul wrote: "Now to each one the manifestation of the Spirit is given for the common good" (1 Corinthians 12:7). This verse indicates that the Spirit's primary objective for the distribution of the gifts is the common good of the Church, rather than the individual believer.

The tendency for those living in individualistic, Western societies is to interpret the gift passages as related to individuals. Yet the Spirit is primarily concerned about the group—in contrast to the individual—and He endows the *charismata* on the Church. The reason that individuals are given free grace in the form of gifts is to bless and edify Christ's Church.

The situational view of the gifts creates a greater expectation for the Holy Spirit to work in new, exciting ways—rather than, for instance, to wait for Harry who has the gift of tongues and always delivers his gift at 10:15 on Sunday morning. The situational view also frees believers from operating only in their one or two gifts and not expecting to be used in any other way, opening the door for new possibilities.

A Balance between Views

My own conviction is that both views are right. I believe that the Holy Spirit can, in His sovereignty, give any believer one of His endowments at any time—even if that gift is not part of the person's usual gift mix. I believe equally, however, that the Spirit normally places one or two dominant gifts in each believer's life.

Paul seemed to indicate the distribution of particular gifts to individuals in Romans 12 when he wrote:

> For by the grace given me I say to every one of you: Do not think of yourself more highly than you ought, but rather think of yourself with sober judgment, in accordance with the measure of faith God has given you. . . . We have different gifts, according to the grace given us. If a man's gift is prophesying, let him use it in proportion to his faith.
>
> verses 3, 6

Paul then went on to talk about additional gifts that the Holy Spirit has distributed to members of the body.

God grants measures of faith and grace, and He also distributes particular gifts. The caution in our over-individualized society is to understand that God is concerned more about the group than the individual when He gives His gifts.

I think that each believer should be open to receiving new *charismata* as the Spirit wills. Does someone need healing? Perhaps God will grant you one of the gifts of healing for a particular moment to meet a particular need. Does someone need specific counsel? Perhaps God will give you the gift of exhortation for that particular occasion. Perhaps suddenly, God will grant you the endowment of teaching to clarify a passage that was way beyond your capability to understand. He might do this occasionally, even though you know in your heart that your primary spiritual gift is service.

It seems that some people go overboard with elaborate gift lists and "foolproof" methods of discovery. It is a better idea to focus on the needs within the Church and then ask, "How has God positioned me to meet those needs?" The exercising of a spiritual gift should bring fulfillment to you, but more importantly, it should minister to others in the Body of Christ.

Identification of the Gifts

Throughout this book, I have declared that the small group is the best place to exercise spiritual gifts. The atmosphere of trust in a small group is the key cornerstone that allows the free flow of the spiritual gifts. When trust is established, people are more willing to risk and try out new, potential gifts. A small group has great potential to provide honest feedback about the person's success, as well as areas of improvement.

Operate in the Context of a Relationship

The only way to discover spiritual gifts is in the context of relationship. Spiritual gift tests, while helping believers to think through the possibilities, are insufficient in themselves. Gift surveys do give a glimpse of how to perceive giftedness, but people can project into those questionnaires the gifts they *want* to have, rather than affirm the gifts they actually have.[9] The more people develop relationships in the context of a group, the better idea they will have concerning their own spiritual giftedness—always remembering that gifts function in the context of relationships. I encourage believers to read material, take one or two gift tests, step out in the exercise of potential spiritual gifts and then seek confirmation from others. Were people edified? Was Christ glorified? When trust is high, members feel that they can experiment with a variety of gifts, and they do not feel thwarted.

In the larger worship service, experimentation with the gifts rarely happens because a larger audience demands a certain level of performance. Risk taking is not encouraged in such an environment, nor should it be. In the safety of the small group and with the encouragement of the group leader, experimentation can happen, and the Holy Spirit will bless.

Although the primary application of spiritual giftedness is found in the Church, I believe the Spirit also wants to use the gifts to reach a lost world. The Spirit can use His endowments through believers at work, at home or at school. Jesus loves the whole world, and He wants to reach it through His Body. Perhaps when you are talking with a friend or colleague at work, a particular need arises. The same Spirit who was at work in your small group the night before wants to use you right then and there. Ask the Spirit to give you wisdom and to manifest His gifts through you, whether they be miracles, discernment of spirits or service.

If you have the gift of mercy, for instance, God will surely use you in hospital visitation, whether or not you are visiting a church member. Those with the gift of evangelism must take their gift to the world at large. Dr. Robert L. Saucy, professor at Talbot Seminary, says, "Since the church is the church whether members are gathered for corporate meeting or scattered in their homes and communities, the ministry of gifts can take place in all situations."[10] The gifts are primarily for the edification of the Church, but the Holy Spirit is pleased to manifest His gifts to needy people, wherever they might be.

Experiment with Various Gifts

Once the group members become comfortable with each other and more knowledgeable about spiritual gifts, the leader can encourage them to confirm in each other their spiritual gifts in the small group time.

The gift that God gives you does not need to be something different from your natural abilities. It might not even appear on the lists (although the lists are certainly good places to start), nor may it be the same gift at all times.

Anything God has given you that you can use to meet a need in the Body can be your spiritual gift. So often, a particular gift springs up in the presence of a particular need: a person with emotional difficulties, a demon-possessed person, a non-Christian with serious questions. In the presence of such needs, the Holy Spirit might endow you with a gifting that you did not know you had (and perhaps, you *did not* have it until that moment!).

Gift discovery takes place in the process of serving one another, caring for one another and living the life of the Body. When you find that God *consistently* blesses your efforts in a certain area, you can conclude confidently that you have that particular gift.

Some churches magnify just one or two gifts to the exclusion of others. Some have called this process "gift colonization." If the pastor is a gifted evangelist with regular campaigns, there may be a strong tendency to organize the entire church around evangelism. The other gifts of the Holy Spirit may be less likely to be manifested in the church because like-minded people will either stay or leave, depending on whether or not they like the pastor.

Great group facilitators, on the other hand, allow for more diversity. The leader needs to be open to allowing people to experiment with gifts that are different from his or her own gift mix—as long as the use of that gift edifies the rest of the group. As the leader gives members more liberty to exercise their gifts, the members will experience a new responsibility and will consequently feel more committed to the church.

Check Your Desire Level

One of the main secrets behind discovering spiritual giftedness is trying to determine your "desire level" to operate in a particular gift. Exercising a gift should not be a chore—it should be enjoyed. You should experience a high degree of passion and desire when exercising your spiritual gifts. I like to ask those trying to identify spiritual giftedness: Do you like explaining biblical truth? Perhaps you have the gift of teaching. Do you enjoy praying for people in the group, and when you do, do you see them healed? Perhaps you have the gift of healing. Do you love to bring refreshments and organize group events? Perhaps you have the gift of helps or administration. Are you drawn to visit cell members who are having problems? Perhaps you have the gift of mercy.

Joy, excitement and fulfillment should accompany the exercise of spiritual gifts. Greg Ogden writes in *The New Reformation*: "The central clue to discovering our spiritual gifts is to get in touch with the spheres of service that produce a flow of inner joy, excitement and energy."[11] When it feels heavy and burdensome to exercise a spiritual gift, it might be because no such gift exists—the person was simply trying to fulfill in the flesh what only the Holy Spirit can do through His *charismata*.

Seek Confirmation from Others

Another key test is confirmation from others. I often tell people to look for confirmation from those in the group. What do people confirm in you? If they notice your capacity to clarify the meaning of Scripture, you may have the gift of teaching. My wife's gift of counseling (exhortation) has been confirmed over and over in the small group environment. The gifts were given for the edification of the Body of Christ, and when you edify someone with your gift, others will let you know.

Releasing Others to Minister

The "Super Leader Syndrome" occurs when the leader thinks that the title *leader* means that he or she must do everything. This is simply not true. The best leaders utilize the giftedness of everyone in the cell. The best leaders recognize that each person in the cell has something to share, and that utilizing the giftedness of each member is essential for the health of the group, as well as the health of each person. The best cell leaders realize that God is pleased when everyone is working together in harmony.

For a long time, I thought that the members of my small group were interested in hearing only me, but then I discovered that they really wanted to hear others besides me! The small group atmosphere is simply too conducive to intimate sharing to regurgitate a sermon, a lecture or a Bible study. The small group is also the perfect training ground for people to learn to use their gifts. In an effective small group, people learn to labor, are equipped for ministry, are encouraged to exercise their gifts and develop vision. Ultimately, they become leaders.

I started my own ministry in a small group. I learned to lead, teach, exhort, administer and, above all, pastor a small group of people. Doubtful potential leaders learn to spread their wings and fly in a small group atmosphere by taking baby steps. Would-be leaders learn through an incremental process of doing and learning.

"Super Leaders" must learn to facilitate others by asking them to get involved. Not only will this make the small group leader's job so much easier, it will also satisfy the needs of the members. Turning members into ministers will involve:

- Teaching on spiritual gifts and then giving opportunities for members to use their gifts
- Creating assignments for group members (such as to pray, to lead worship, to bring refreshments, to evangelize neighbors)
- Rotating the small group location so that different members have a chance to host

- Taking turns in facilitating the small group lesson, allowing specific gifts to be manifested
- Evangelistic outreach from the small group, in which various gifts, including the gift of evangelism, will be revealed

Allowing small group participation is always risky. When people and emotions are involved, a certain amount of messiness cannot be avoided. Yet life and joy are also generated, which makes the difficult moments more than worthwhile. As Paul said about the Holy Spirit, "Now the Lord is the Spirit, and where the Spirit of the Lord is, there is freedom" (2 Corinthians 3:17). We need to allow the Holy Spirit to bring that same freedom into our groups and allow Him to work through each member.

7

SERVICE AND EQUIPPING GIFTS

When attempting to define the specific gifts of the Spirit, a certain amount of humility is called for. After all, the writers of the New Testament gave us very little information about each particular gift. Some modern writers on spiritual gifts boldly describe each gift in exact detail, when in reality, the New Testament data might only give a sentence or less concerning what that gift actually involves.

I am confident that all of the gifts of the Spirit are active in Christ's Church today. Some people teach that "word gifts"—such as miracles, prophecy, tongues and the interpretation of tongues—ceased with the apostles; in other words, they believe that supernatural gifts were only needed until the New Testament canon was completed.

I believe that the New Testament record of spiritual gifts is just as active, real and relevant today in the 21st century as it was in the first century. The length and focus of this book does not allow me to go into detail about why I believe all of the gifts of the Spirit are active today, but to read more on this topic, I highly recommend the book *Are Miraculous Gifts for Today?* edited by Wayne A. Grudem.[1]

Repeatedly in my small group ministry, I hear of burdened leaders who feel as if they do not have enough time to fulfill all the responsibilities of small group leadership. When probing further, I often notice that these leaders have not mobilized the giftedness of the people in their groups: It has become a one-man or one-woman show. In contrast, the best small group leaders delegate frequently. These great leaders see their small groups come alive with gifted people who really want to be used.

The three general categories of gifts include service, equipping, and prayer and worship gifts. We will discuss the prayer and worship category of gifts in the two chapters that follow.

The Service Gifts

Service gifts abound in Christ's Church today. Many believers have one of the service gifts, and small group leaders need to perceive who has been gifted with administration (see 1 Corinthians 12:28), helps (see 1 Corinthians 12:28), giving (see Romans 12:8), mercy (see Romans 12:8), service (see Romans 12:7) and faith (see 1 Corinthians 12:9).

Administration/Organization

Paul talks about those with the gift of administration in 1 Corinthians 12:28, but it can also be seen in Exodus 18:13–27. The Greek word for *administration* in this verse can also be translated as "steerer." In ancient times, the one who steered a ship was under orders of the captain. The captain charted out the course, and the steerer followed the directions. The steerer's role involved working out the specific details in order to arrive safely at port—the destination the captain had chosen.

The word *organization* is also used to describe this gift. Those with the gift of administration love to plan and organize ministry events. The Holy Spirit blesses people with this gift so that ideas will be carried out practically rather than haphazardly.

When our small group decided to take a camping trip, Riza Hassell, a member of the group, volunteered to organize everything. She felt called to do this. Her spiritual gifting prompted her to take phone numbers, plan meals and organize schedules. We did ask her to allow for flexibility and told her that we wanted a lot of free time on the trip. (The danger of this gift can be seen when a person wants to over-organize.)

Helps

This is the Spirit-given ability to give practical assistance that will encourage other believers to fulfill their responsibilities (see Exodus 18:21–22; Numbers 11:16–17). Those with the gift of helps lighten the load of other believers. Epaphroditus practiced this gift in Philippians 2:25 when he attended to Paul's personal needs.

To avoid burnout, small group facilitators need to discern which members of the group have this endowment of the Holy Spirit. Many members are inwardly saying, *Please use me*, but because facilitators do not want to over-burden busy people, the tendency is not to ask. Because the gift of helps is a Spirit-inspired gift, the Holy Spirit will stir people to want to help—and to do it with the proper motivation.

People with the gift of helps will gladly make phone calls, visit other people, bring refreshments and generally help lighten the load of the leader. I believe that God has freely poured out this gift in small group ministry so that the leader does not experience burnout. Those with the gift of helps will often serve by planning for small group activities.

Giving

The gift of giving is a Spirit-endowed *charismata* that stirs a person to share money both generously and cheerfully (see Luke 3:11; 21:1–4; John 12:3–8; Acts 4:32–37; 20:35; Romans 12:8; 2 Corinthians 8:2–5). People with this gift usually give significantly beyond the normal tithe, which I believe should be the minimum starting point for believers. Those with the gift of giving do not ask, "How much do I have to give to God?" Instead, they joyfully turn this question around by asking, "How much does God want me to keep?" Some people with this gift even give more to God's work than they keep for themselves.

If the small group facilitator has this gift, he or she will probably mobilize the group to give to the poor, bless those in need and look for opportunities to bless others. Group members with this gift will cheerfully try to meet the physical needs of those in the group. Because those in the small group know each other so well, when needs arise, those with the gift of giving joyfully seek to meet those needs.

Mercy

The person with the gift of mercy senses God's compassion for neglected people (those on the edge of society) in a special way (see Matthew 25:37–40; Mark 9:41; Luke 10:33–37; Acts 9:36–42; Romans 12:8; James 1:27; 2:14–17). Those with the gift of mercy do not simply offer words of encouragement; they give practical aid to people who are troubled in mind, body or spirit. Those with this gift often have a ministry to the handicapped, the elderly, the mentally disabled and drug addicts.

The facilitator with the gift of mercy will encourage outreach to those on the edge of society. But the fact that the facilitator has a burden for these people does not mean that the members will. Facilitators with this gift must work hard to prepare their members to reach out to others.

The beauty of small group ministry is its homogenous flexibility. Spirit-filled groups can fit different sizes and mixes according to the giftedness of the leader and members. Mike, a small group leader in Big Bear, California, with a gift of mercy, leads a group geared toward those devastated by alcohol. It happened quite naturally as alcoholic friends invited their friends. All of these people needed to be healed in the small group before they would ever darken the door of the Sunday morning service. Yet after several months, Mike told me excitedly that the entire group showed up in church one Sunday.

Service

The word for the gift of service is *diakonos*, which means "minister" or "servant" and from which we get our word *deacon* (see Luke 10:38–42; 22:24–27; Acts 6:1–7; Romans 12:7; 1 Timothy 3:8–13). In Acts 6:2–4, the apostles asked the multitude to choose Spirit-filled ministers, so that they would have more time to seek the Lord and care for the flock.

Christian Schwarz, researcher and author, discovered that 81 percent who had the gift of service also had the gift of helps, and that these two gifts were most frequently paired together.[2] The Holy Spirit has blessed the Church with an abundant supply of people who are willing to serve and willing to help, because the Holy Spirit has anointed these people with the desire to do so. Ron Nichols, a small group leader, provides a personal example of how the gift of service works in the small group context:

> When my car failed to start once in ten-below-zero winter weather, Steve and Cathy [a couple in our Koinonia group at church] loaned me their brand-new car so that I could drive to work. When my wife, Jill, returned from the hospital with our new twin girls, we enjoyed several meals brought in by members of the same small group. We cried together when one member told of a car accident and problems at work. We all feel the pain when a couple's child is in the hospital.[3]

Faith

The gift of faith is the Spirit-enabled ability to recognize what God wants to do in an impossible situation and then to trust Him to get that task accomplished (see Matthew 8:5–13; 17:20; 21:18–22; Romans 4:18–21; 1 Corinthians

12:9; James 1:5–8). Certainly, everyone has been given a measure of faith, but God has blessed some people with the capacity to envision—with confidence—what God is going to do in His Church.

Paul exemplified this gift of faith on the ship to Rome. Everyone had given up hope, and the ship itself seemed ready to sink. Yet Paul's faith grew ever brighter. He emerged from his spiritual retreat and proclaimed that God's Word would be fulfilled and that everyone would be saved. God triumphed in the situation, just as Paul had been assured that He would—even in the face of dark obstacles (see Acts 27:22–44).

Examples of this gift in history are also plentiful. George Mueller (1805–1898) felt God calling him to take care of orphaned children, but God also showed him how to do so without ever asking for money. It is estimated that Mueller cared for ten thousand orphans by faith alone over a sixty-year period. One morning, for example, with no food on hand, Mueller prayed, "Father, we thank Thee for the food Thou art going to give us." Suddenly there was a knock on the door. It was the baker, who said he had awakened at two in the morning and felt the need to give bread. A few minutes later, the milkman arrived, saying that his truck had broken down and that the milk would spoil unless the orphanage took it. This and countless other miracles occurred as Mueller trusted God.[4] Hudson Taylor, missionary to China, possessed a similar gift.

Small group leaders who possess this gift of faith see possibilities of growth and blessing when others are ready to give up. They see the invisible realm when everyone else is caught up in doubt, disappointment and tough circumstances.

Gehazi saw the Syrian armies surrounding the Israelites, but Elisha saw the great host of angels who far outnumbered the Syrian armies (see 2 Kings 6:15–19). Those with the gift of faith see the glass as being half full rather than half empty. And their sight is not worked up by positive mantras. Instead, the Spirit fills their minds with a greater, more real way of looking at life.

Sometimes the Holy Spirit will give the gift of faith to a small group member to encourage a doubtful facilitator. The good news is that the Holy Spirit knows what each group needs, and He grants His gifts to small groups in order to bring balance among the people.

The Equipping Gifts

The equipping gifts help lay a strong foundation in the small group. The Holy Spirit often manifests Himself through the gift of exhortation (see Romans 12:8), wisdom and knowledge (see 1 Corinthians 12:8), teaching (see 1 Corinthians 12:28), pastoring (see Ephesians 4:11), apostleship (see 1 Corinthians 12:28; Ephesians 4:11), evangelism (see Ephesians 4:11) and leadership (see Romans 12:8).

Exhortation/Counseling

The Greek word for "exhortation" in its noun form is *paraclete*, which means, "one who is called alongside to comfort and counsel" (see John 4:1–42; Acts 14:21–22; Romans 12:8; 2 Corinthians 1:3–7; 1 Thessalonians 2:11; 5:14; 1 Timothy 5:1). Jesus used this same word in John 14:16 when He called the Holy Spirit "another Counselor."

Most people believe that Barnabas possessed the gift of exhortation because he was able not only to build up Paul but also to counsel others to see the potential in Paul. Most of the disciples at that time were deathly afraid of Saul—even after his conversion. Before his encounter with Christ, he had terrorized them, taking joy in dragging them off to prison. Yet Barnabas's gift of exhortation allowed the disciples to see Paul in a different light. The Scriptures say that "Barnabas took him [Paul] and brought him to the apostles" (Acts 9:27).

Many people identify the gift of exhortation with counseling because it includes a God-given ability and wisdom to help people change. A great counselor is patient, willing to listen and able to impart solid scriptural advice. Yet those with the gift of exhortation are also willing to confront and challenge.

True love goes the extra mile and helps people change. *Care-fronting* is a term referring to those who care and will speak the truth in love. Urging people to action is part of the counselor's role. The apostle Paul urged people to act: "So I thought it necessary to urge the brothers to visit you in advance and finish the arrangements for the generous gift you had promised" (2 Corinthians 9:5).

When members use the gift of exhortation in the small group context, they offer Spirit-anointed counsel out of a concerned heart. Often they continue to use their gift of exhortation outside the small group.

Wisdom

In 1 Corinthians 12:8, Paul wrote: "To one there is given through the Spirit the message of wisdom" (see also 1 Kings 3:5–28; 1 Corinthians 12:7; James

3:13–18). It seems that the Holy Spirit specifically grants this gift to certain people who are able to apply God's wisdom to various situations. Such people are regularly able to offer Spirit-anointed advice and, more specifically, God's Word, in a wide variety of situations. Those with the gift of wisdom can be compared to a physician who offers a diagnosis and then applies medical research to an individual's illness.

When someone expresses a problem or crisis during a small group meeting, it is good to listen carefully and then allow others to respond. The Holy Spirit will often stir someone who has the gift of wisdom to offer the right answer. But even if no one with this gift is present, I still recommend that the small group leader stop for a moment and say, "Let's pray and ask for wisdom. Let's claim the promise found in James 1:5: 'If any of you lacks wisdom, he should ask God, who gives generously to all without finding fault, and it will be given to him.'" After the prayer, confidently ask the rest of the group what the Holy Spirit has shown them. Often someone who has been given the message of wisdom will speak forth a God-given answer to the situation.

Many people equate the *word of wisdom* with the *word of knowledge.* That is, they believe that it is a momentary, supernatural gift that God gives to people. I have described this phenomenon in my discussion of the gift of prophecy in the next chapter.

Knowledge

The gift of knowledge is probably the most difficult gift to define (see Romans 15:14; 1 Corinthians 8:1–2; 12:8; 13:2, 8–10; 2 Corinthians 12:7; Ephesians 3:14–

19). Much of the confusion stems from the fact that Paul does not describe this gift in much detail. Many people believe that the gift of knowledge, as Paul described it in 1 Corinthians 12:8, is a momentary insight, image or vision that a person then speaks forth. I certainly do encourage such manifestations, but I would classify these bursts of knowledge or visions as an aspect of the gift of prophecy. I would consider a person to be prophesying when, in the group, he or she says, "I'm receiving an impression from the Lord that . . ." I would also consider a person to be operating in the prophetic gift when he or she says, "The Lord is showing me that someone is getting healed in the left shoulder." Some people label this as a word of knowledge; again, I would classify it as a subset of prophecy.

In 1 Corinthians 14, Paul described the gift of prophecy at length, even telling believers to desire this gift. The person who prophesies speaks to men for their strengthening, encouragement and comfort (see 14:3). Most of the time, this is exactly what people do when they speak forth a word of knowledge. I have noticed, however, that some people have a God-given ability to do research. I believe the *gift* of knowledge better describes the Spirit-endowment that God gives certain people to collect and analyze knowledge from a wide variety of sources, and then to apply that knowledge through writing, teaching and preaching. In my opinion, this is the gift of knowledge to which Paul is referring.

It is great when a small group contains members with the gift of knowledge who can serve as a resource to clarify doubts or answer questions. Great turmoil happens, however, when someone with the gift of knowledge also has the gift of gab. Those with the gift of knowledge must pray to learn how to listen to others proactively.

Teaching

The Holy Spirit endows the gift of teaching upon believers so that they might clarify God's Word to the people (see Acts 18:24–28; Romans 12:7; 1 Corinthians 12:28–29; Ephesians 4:11–14; James 3:1). Those with the gift of teaching have the ability to clarify and simplify, and they are confirmed by the fact that people truly learn from them. Those with the gift of teaching focus on the questions of their listeners, rather than expounding on theory after theory that only has relevance to the teacher, not to the hearers. This gift is listed third in the biblical order (see 1 Corinthians 12:28), and is found in all three gift passages (see Romans 12:7; Ephesians 4:11). The gift of exhortation urges a person to do the work, but those with the gift of teaching tell people *how* to do the work.

A teacher exercising his or her gift in a classroom setting clarifies a particular topic through a mix of speaking and group dynamics, with the goal of imparting knowledge to the student. This form of teaching is important, and most small group-based churches around the world make extensive use of gifted teachers to train those in small groups.

If the small group facilitator has the gift of teaching, he or she will have a special ability to prepare excellent questions that stir the members to learn what the biblical text really means. One small group leader named Alfred certainly possessed the gift of teaching. Alfred prepared fervently all week for his Thursday night group. At the time I knew Alfred, I did not understand much about small group ministry, and I fully expected a Bible study, complete with exegesis, opinions from various commentators and illustrations. Yet Alfred spoke very little that night, instead skillfully drawing the information from us. Although he had scrutinized the Bible passage himself, he led us to dig up the treasures for ourselves. He peppered us with questions that forced us to delve deeper and deeper into the text. I left that meeting with a new appreciation for the powerful learning dynamic of active participation in studying God's Word. I also discovered that diligent lesson preparation and open sharing are not mutually exclusive. Alfred empowered our small group to discover God's Word for ourselves.

The small group facilitator who has the gift of teaching must make sure that he or she is only talking thirty percent of the time, and is allowing those in the small group to participate seventy percent of the time. The grave danger in this situation is for the facilitator to turn the small group into a classroom lecture.

Those members of the small group who have the gift of teaching will have the special ability to clarify the Word of God in a clear, understandable way. Members of the small group with the gift of teaching must work hard on listening to others and not dominating. They must learn that silence in the small group is not an invitation for them to launch into a teaching lecture. Most of the time, the small group member with the gift of teaching will share personal insight from Scripture as it applies to the lesson.

Leadership

Those with the gift of leadership often have a following (see Exodus 18:13–27; Romans 12:8; 1 Thessalonians 5:12–13; 1 Timothy 3:1–7; 5:17–25). People follow true leaders not because they are coerced or pressured—but because they want to. Great leaders influence and inspire people to expect great things from God and attempt great things for God. The person with the gift of leadership does not necessarily need to have a particular office (such as a pastor, elder or apostle). Other people will respect the gift of leadership whether the person is officially in charge or not. In Romans 12:8, Paul added that those with the gift of leadership must lead with diligence. The Greek word for "diligence" in this verse is *spoude* and means "speed in carrying out a matter." It is just the opposite of slothfulness. Anyone exercising leadership must be diligent.

It is not necessary to have the gift of leadership in order to facilitate a small group. The best small group leaders depend on God and marshal the giftedness of everyone in the group. It certainly does not hurt, however, for a facilitator to have this gift. Facilitators who have this gift will offer clear-cut direction to the group with regard to evangelism and multiplication. Facilitators who are not endowed with this gift should encourage members with the gift of leadership to participate in the small group—by leading worship, teaching the lesson, directing evangelistic outreach or even heading up the new leadership team when the group is ready to multiply.

Pastoring/Shepherding

This gift is the Spirit-given ability to care for and feed a group of believers (see John 10:1–15; Acts 20:28–31; Ephesians 4:11; 1 Thessalonians 5:12–13; 1 Timothy 4:11–16; Hebrews 13:7, 17, 20–21; 1 Peter 5:1–5). It also involves protecting that group of believers from error. Paul exhorted the shepherds at Ephesus: "Keep watch over yourselves and all the flock of which the Holy Spirit has made you overseers. Be shepherds of the church of God, which he bought with his own blood" (Acts 20:28). It is important to distinguish between the roles of pastor and elder—which are used interchangeably—with the gift of shepherding. It is one thing to fill the role of pastor or elder, but it is quite another to have the gift of pastoring. Those with the gift of pastoring might work at a computer company, while the official full-time pastor might not actually have the gift of pastoring. It is not necessary, in other words, to have the gift of pastoring in order to be an effective pastor.

God has blessed both men and women with the gift of shepherding. The small group is a great place to use this gift because of the hands-on care and personal involvement a small group often requires. If the facilitator has the gift of shepherding, he or she will strongly emphasize pastoral care, visitation and personal ministry. The danger, however, would be not to sufficiently emphasize other areas such as evangelism, outreach and leadership development that results in multiplication.

Small group facilitators should remain alert for members with the gift of shepherding. Those with this gift can mentor new believers, visit the sick and meet one-on-one with small group members who are hurting. Small groups are often the springboard for one-on-one relationships that happen outside the normal small group meeting. A grave error among small group leaders is the assumption that they have to be the ones to develop all the relationships. Such thinking is the sure path to burnout. Those with the gift of shepherding can help tremendously in the edification of the small group.

Apostleship

This gift is in no way limited to the original twelve apostles, because the New Testament recognizes additional apostles beyond the Twelve. This gift has normally been applied to church planters like the apostle Paul, who pioneered new territories for the Gospel (see Matthew 10:2–15; John 13:12–17; Acts 8:14–25; 14:14–15; 15:1–6; Romans 16:7; 1 Corinthians 12:28–29; 2 Corinthians 12:12; Galatians 1:1; Ephesians 4:11). I believe that the Holy Spirit manifests this gift in people who are recognized as spiritual leaders by a variety of churches, and whose authority extends beyond the local church. In the Greek language, the word *apostle* is a nautical term that refers to an admiral over a fleet of ships, which, under orders from a ruler, would start a colony. Such chosen apostles would have great authority and would travel extensively to foreign lands. In the New Testament, apostles were commissioned to start churches.[5]

Someone with the gift of apostleship might lead a small group to keep in touch with the sheep. I recommend this. Far too often, an apostle cannot relate to ordinary believers with real-life problems; an apostle's ministry would be enhanced by either leading a small group or regularly attending one. If the apostle is a member of a small group, he must not dominate, but instead share transparently about his weaknesses, just like everyone else. Those with the gift of apostleship must be accountable to other believers, and small groups are the best way to make sure this happens.

Evangelism

Those with the gift of evangelism are able both to communicate the Gospel to nonbelievers and lead them to Jesus (see Acts 8:5–6; 8:26–40; 14:13–21; Romans 10:14–15; Ephesians 4:11). Peter Wagner and David Cho have insisted for years that approximately ten percent of believers have this gift, and new research confirms this fact.[6] Ephesians 4:11 talks about the role of the evangelist, and it assumes that an evangelist would have the gift of evangelism.

If the small group facilitator has the gift of evangelism, the group will grow quickly through conversion growth. It is essential that those with the gift of shepherding and teaching marshal their gifts to disciple the new believers. The facilitator must set a multiplication date quickly, because when a small group grows to over fifteen adults, the group almost immediately loses intimacy, and people stop coming back. Members with the gift of evangelism are a godsend to the small group. It is important, however, that philosophical harmony exist between the facilitator and the evangelist, and that both are working together to extend Christ's Kingdom.

8

THE WORSHIP GIFTS

I remember when Harold Weitz asked Celyce and me
to come forward in front of the one thousand participants of a cell church conference held in South Africa
in 1999. We knew that Pastor Harold was well-known
for his prophetic gifts, but we were not expecting to
receive a prophecy before a thousand other people. His
prophecy for us lasted almost five minutes! One small
part of the word was this:

> Now, know this today, this is the hour, says God, that you
> will go forth, and a new mantle falls on this night for you;
> this is your experience of the burning bush that you've
> waited for; this is the experience, says the Lord, for from
> this night, I will cause you not to rest, and you will move
> endlessly and tirelessly. As my servant Paul, says the Lord,
> the same kind of anointing will rest on your life.

Immediately after he prophesied over us, I preached, just as I had done each of the previous three nights. But something was different this time. I saw Jesus in a new way. I felt His control and power. It was no longer Joel Comiskey standing up to preach after practicing incessantly for hours. My burdens lifted. Jesus became so real that night that I felt as though I could touch Him—just as He had been so real when He first touched me and healed my life back in 1973. My words flowed effortlessly. I was no longer trying to impress the group; Jesus flowed through me. It was His work, and not my own.

I bought the tape and wrote down every word of Harold's prophecy. I still reread it on occasion when I need encouragement. And this is the purpose of prophecy—encouragement, joy and strength. The Holy Spirit uses prophecy to edify His Church, not to tear it down.

In this chapter, I will cover the worship and prayer gifts. These gifts include prophecy (see 1 Corinthians 12:10), tongues (see 1 Corinthians 12:10), the interpretation of tongues (see 1 Corinthians 12:10), healing (see 1 Corinthians 12:9), miracles (see 1 Corinthians 12:10) and the discernment of spirits (see 1 Corinthians 12:10).

Prophecy

The gift of prophecy is the God-given gifting to receive a message from God and then to speak it forth to His Church (see Deuteronomy 13:1–5; 18:18–22; 1 Samuel 3:1–21; Matthew 7:15–20; 24:11, 23–24; Acts 15:32; 1 Corinthians 12:28–29; 14:3, 22–40; 2 Peter 1:19–21; 1 John 4:1–6; Revelation 1:1–3). This is an important gift to small group ministry, because the Holy Spirit uses it to manifest His presence, assuring people that He is alive and talking directly to them.

Some people think that the gift of prophecy only re-lates to future revelation. This is not true. Far more prophecies deal with present realities than with future visions. The Greek word *prophesy* simply means "to speak forth." Those who speak forth have received a personal message from God that applies to a concrete situation. The Spirit of God then takes over the message and directs it to the larger Body.

This gift will never contradict the inerrant Word of God, although it does bring new information that is transmitted from God to human beings. Unfortunately, because those who are communicating God's message remain sinful human beings, sometimes the message from God is skewed—this is why discernment is needed. The Scriptures tell us that we should always test the prophecies to make sure they are in line with Scripture (see 1 Corinthians 14:29–33).

Prophecy and preaching are not the same thing. It is one thing to depend on the Spirit when you are preach-ing; it is another thing to have the Spirit take over while you are preaching and to speak new words. Prophecy requires no preparation, but great preaching requires a great deal of practice.

Inspirational Prophecy

The goal of inspirational prophecy is to inspire God's people and to build them up in the faith, and this type of prophecy does not usually contain revelation of any kind. The simplest form of prophecy might be similar to Mary's proclamation, "My soul glorifies the Lord" (Luke

145

1:46), or one of King David's prayers that later became a psalm. It seems that Paul had inspirational prophecy in mind when he wrote: "Everyone who prophesies speaks to men for their strengthening, encouragement and comfort" (1 Corinthians 14:3).

This kind of prophecy is within the grasp of many believers and should be encouraged in the small group setting. Paul, in fact, said that believers should desire the spiritual gifts—especially the gift of prophecy (1 Corinthians 14:1). It is a great privilege to be a vessel of the Holy Spirit to other believers. Because the New Testament was written to believers who were meeting in house churches, the natural setting for prophecy is the small group experience. Either after or during worship is a great time for the small group leader to pause and ask if God is impressing any of the members to share a message to edify the rest of the group.

Kirk, a multiplication leader from my own small group, regularly prophesies, and he also encourages other people to step out on their impressions. On more than one occasion he has said: "When giving a prophecy, I like to always start by saying, 'I think the Holy Spirit is saying to me' or 'I believe this is what He's saying.'" Kirk realizes that human beings can make mistakes—and that he is no exception. Kirk believes that all prophecy must have the goal of edifying the Body.

Small groups are a great place to hear the voice of God and experience God's power in a new, dynamic way. In the loving atmosphere of a home group, especially where the gifts are working and where the Holy Spirit is operating, people grow in ministry and serving others.

Nonbelievers and the Prophetic Word

Inspirational prophecy does not apply only to believers; it applies to nonbelievers as well. The Holy Spirit empowers His Church with gifts such as prophecy to reach nonbelievers, as well as to edify Christians.

When the Holy Spirit speaks through the Body of Christ, nonbelievers will be attracted to the reality of a God who is alive and who speaks today. So much of traditional church life is based on the marvelous things that God did in years past. But people yearn to experience His life and power today.

The term *power evangelism* is often used to describe the reaching of nonbelievers through the demonstration of God's reality *today*—just like what occurred in the book of Acts. Paul the apostle wrote: "Our gospel came to you not simply with words, but also with power, with the Holy Spirit and with deep conviction" (1 Thessalonians 1:5). This method of witnessing has also been called *worship evangelism*.[1] Truly, the most powerful attraction that we can offer nonbelievers is God Himself. When an unbeliever enters a group that is fully moving in the gifts of the Spirit and exalting Christ in their midst, that person will be convinced that God is real, alive and eager to speak to him or her personally—today.

Prophecy plays a key role in ministering to nonbelievers in the small group setting. First Corinthians 14:24–25 brings this out:

> If an unbeliever or someone who does not understand comes in while everybody is prophesying, he will be convinced by all that he is a sinner and will be judged by all, and the se-

147

crets of his heart will be laid bare. So he will fall down and worship God, exclaiming, "God is really among you!"

A careful examination of the context of these verses reveals that Paul was writing to a house church, since literally *everyone* present was able to prophesy. If everyone were to prophesy, it would have to have been a group small enough to allow everyone to speak. The word *prophesy* in this passage refers to "speaking forth truth."[2] Paul was saying that *everyone* would be able to speak words of edification and exhortation and comfort. Those who were prophesying were ministering words of edification and encouragement as the Holy Spirit led them.[3]

When a person in the small group discloses a need, there is suddenly a reason to minister. Spiritual gifts are exercised when there is a need. When no needs are present, people do not feel an urgency to use their gifts and minister to others. But when a need arises, suddenly everyone wants to get involved—and this is exciting. As each person begins to minister to and love those around him, there is a new sense of power and anointing.

Many small group leaders seem to think that the presence of non-Christians will hinder the flow of a community, but my experience is that just the opposite occurs. When non-Christians enter the room, there is a new flow, a new zeal, a new desire to share. Having God near is very important in small group ministry. The Spirit is the one who gives the supernatural power and grace needed to penetrate a lost world for Jesus. All of the gifts of the Spirit are the inheritance of the entire Body of Christ.

Two visitors came to our small group one night. We knew that one of them was a nonbeliever, and we were not sure about the other person's relationship to Christ. Even with the visitors in the group, we continued the normal order of meeting, knowing that the best form of evangelism was the Holy Spirit's presence. Eventually, one of the small group members asked if he could share an impression with those who were present. He turned to the single mother who had come for the first time, and said, "Could I share something with you?" and then he proceeded to tell her that Jesus loved her and saw no shame in her life.

My eyes filled with tears because his word was so totally on the mark. What the person who prophesied did not know was that this woman had felt a great deal of shame, having never married the father of her only child. She did not feel accepted in many circles, but to suddenly have God Himself speak to her in such a way touched her heart deeply. God showed up in the small group setting, and she left changed and excited about God again.

Both of our visitors were touched in the small group during that meeting. The other visitor shared her needs with one of the members during the refreshment time. She was about to move to San Francisco and she was fearful of what that would entail. Our small group member did not want to see this woman leave without Christ in her heart. The unbeliever said she wanted to pray to receive Christ, and several people from the group gathered around her to pray.

Revelatory Prophecy

Those who prophesied in the Bible heard God's voice in a variety of ways: through visions, dreams, audible voices and ecstatic trances.[4] At times, God would reveal a future event, a hidden sin or a new direction through these prophecies. Revelatory prophecy is an exciting form of the gift of prophecy that involves a revelation, a disclosing of information, of some kind.

I believe that what many authors call the *word of knowledge* or the *word of wisdom* is actually a form of revelatory prophecy—for two reasons. First, certain members of the Body of Christ have obviously been anointed by God to do research and to bless the Church with what they have learned as they write, teach and preach. This Holy Spirit gifting seems to better fit the *gift of knowledge* that Paul wrote of in 1 Corinthians 12:8.

Second, what most people call the gift of knowledge or the gift of wisdom has the same function, or purpose, as the gift of revelatory prophecy. That is, someone receives an impression, special knowledge or wisdom or perhaps a dream from God and then communicates it to someone else. In revelatory prophecy, the prophet receives an impression, a word, a dream or a vision, but the connecting point is always Holy Spirit-inspired revelation. I agree with Peter Wagner when he says, "Authors have a very difficult time distinguishing between the gift of knowledge, the gift of wisdom and the gift of prophecy. The three appear to be almost synonymous in their writing."[5] Thus, under the broad category of revelatory prophecy, I am including words of knowledge, words of wisdom, images and visions.

There are some people who have excelled in revelatory prophecy— Pat Robertson and Kathryn Kuhlman, to name just two. Pat Robertson uses this gift regularly. A woman in California, for example, was once watching *The 700 Club* while in a great deal of discomfort from a broken ankle encased in a cast. While on the air, Robertson stated that a woman in a cast was watching the program—and that she had broken her ankle, but God was healing her. In a burst of faith in her spirit, this woman immediately knew that those words had been spoken just for her. Robertson said, "She rose from the chair, removed the cast and with increasing confidence, began to put weight on the broken foot and then to jump on it. The ankle bone had been healed."[6]

At times, the Holy Spirit chooses to bless people by revealing knowledge not naturally available to a messenger. Such knowledge is not intended for gratification, but for edification. There are times when such insight does not come by a direct statement, but by means of a vision or picture that brings immediate illumination. The Holy Spirit might reveal a fact concerning a situation about which the messenger had no previous knowledge. An example of this is when God reveals exact details of a person's life in order to reveal sin, to warn, to provide safety, to reveal thoughts, to provide healing or to provide instruction. A word of knowledge is a special insight and understanding of God and His will concerning the Church and its ministry to a believer. This revelatory prophecy is not "knowledge" in the sense of acquired data, but a specific grasp of certain information that is not "natural," or "worldly."

In our small group one night, we talked about biblical community and the need to walk transparently before God and others. During the prayer time at the end, Justin began to prophesy:

> I saw a stairway with light at the end of it. There were two people walking up the staircase, and one of them had a torch in his hands. He was guiding the other person up the stairway to the top. I believe that God will show us what this means tonight.

Justin then shared with the group how he felt that God was going to touch someone in a special way that night.

The effective small group leader will bask in the Word of God before the group begins, in order to be open to whatever God wants to do through the group. In such an atmosphere, God will often show up with His agenda for the group—an agenda full of grace and mercy.

Because prophecy is a human report of a divine revelation, the "human" aspect of revelatory prophecy is not always right. Prophecy is always based on spontaneous revelation that includes four factors. First, there is the revelation from God. Second, there is the need to understand the revelation. Third, the prophet must interpret what the revelation means, and fourth, the message must be applied correctly.

Only the first factor is ever one hundred percent from God. The second, third and fourth aspects require the action and interpretation of the prophet—who is human and can make mistakes. For this reason, Paul told the Church to test prophecy, saying, "Two or three prophets should speak, and the others should weigh carefully what is said" (1 Corinthians 14:29). Any prophet that resists such testing should be ignored.

Prophets in Paul's day occasionally made mistakes. In Acts 21, a prophet named Agabus approached Paul and his companions. Agabus grabbed Paul's belt, tied his own hands and feet with it and said, "The Holy Spirit says, 'In this way the Jews of Jerusalem will bind the owner of this belt and will hand him over to the Gentiles'" (verse 11). It seems that Agabus and those who accompanied him then tried to persuade Paul not to go to Jerusalem, even though Paul knew that God wanted him to go there. Paul resisted their overtures saying, "Why are you weeping and breaking my heart? I am ready not only to be bound, but also to die in Jerusalem for the name of the Lord Jesus" (verse 13). Agabus's prophecy was right on, but the application was off.

A certain amount of humility must accompany the prophetic word. Sometimes believers forget that the Holy Spirit wants to build up and not tear down. More than one prophetic utterance, for example, has torn people down, made them feel fearful or demanded an immediate decision. John Bevere, a Pentecostal minister, warns in his book *Thus Saith the Lord?* to test each prophetic word and make sure it lines up with the inerrant Word of God. Bevere noticed that prophetic utterances that are not tested in the light of Scripture have the potential to destroy rather than build (for example, prophecies that instruct a person to switch jobs or to marry so and so). Discouragement and even despair can result later when the person discovers that God did not actually speak.[7]

Because of the possibility for error, much of the Church today has chosen to ignore the prophetic word. Yet Paul clearly said, "Do not put out the Spirit's fire; do not treat prophecies with contempt. Test everything. Hold on to the good" (1 Thessalonians 5:19–21). The Holy Spirit wants to speak to His Church through the prophetic word. Those with the gift of prophecy should be encouraged to practice this gift, and the small group is a great place to begin to do so.

Tongues

The gift of tongues is the Holy Spirit's enabling a believer to receive and to speak a divine utterance in

153

a language unknown to him or her (see Mark 16:17; Acts 2:1–13; 10:44–48; 19:1–7; Romans 8:26–27; 1 Corinthians 12:10, 28–30; 14:4–6, 26–28). The gift of speaking in tongues is demonstrated in two different settings: in personal prayer or in public utterance. When using the gift of tongues in public, there should always be an interpreter (see 1 Corinthians 14:27–28). The primary value of tongues is that it is a form of prayer inspired by the Holy Spirit (see 1 Corinthians 14:2), and the gifted person who speaks privately in a tongue edifies himself (see 1 Corinthians 14:4).

The gift of tongues has been a blessing in my own prayer life. Often when I am struggling with a deep problem that I cannot express verbally in prayer, I will speak in tongues. Although I do not understand the language, I realize that the Holy Spirit is speaking through me and that my prayer is going directly to God's throne. Although I enjoy the gift of tongues, I do not consider myself "more spiritual" than other Christians because I speak in tongues—and I rarely talk about this gift. One of my favorite books on the gifts of the Spirit is called *Gift Giver: The Holy Spirit for Today*, written by Craig Keener, a Southern Baptist professor at Eastern Seminary. Keener writes:

> One can pray in tongues yet avoid the controversy. In the circles in which I move, most believers—including those of us who pray in tongues—treat tongues as simply one gift among many useful resources for prayer . . . tongues comes up rarely in my work as a biblical scholar (it appears clearly in only six chapters in the Bible).[8]

If the small group facilitator has the gift of tongues, I recommend that he or she pray in tongues before the group begins in order to receive renewed power. As I mentioned previously, effective small group leaders bask in God's presence and allow themselves to receive His fullness. Tongues is another gift that the Holy Spirit gives to believers in order to prepare them for anointed ministry. In the small group, if someone speaks out in tongues, it should be interpreted either by the person speaking in tongues or by someone else in the group— otherwise real edification is not taking place.

Interpretation of Tongues

The gift of interpretation of tongues is the special ability that God bestows on certain believers to take a message communicated in tongues and make it known in a commonly understood language (see 1 Corinthians 12:10; 12:27–31; 14:1–5, 12–19, 26–28). Often those who interpret also have been given the gift of tongues or prophecy. Quite often, the person who speaks in tongues is even the one who interprets his or her own tongue! What is most important, however, is that someone does interpret the gift of tongues given in a public meeting. Paul made it clear that a public message in tongues is meaningless without an interpretation (see 1 Corinthians 14:27–28). In the same passage, Paul clarified the gift of interpretation and the gift of prophecy, and they seem to have similar characteristics.

Some have pointed out that, unlike prophecy, interpretation is always directed to God, because the Bible says that he who speaks in an unknown tongue speaks directly to God (see 1 Corinthians 14:2). I do not consider this always to be true; I have heard interpretations in both formats.

In the small group setting, the facilitator should instruct those with the gift of tongues that the public gift of tongues always requires an interpretation. The facilitator might even want to explain that anyone who wants to give a message in tongues should pray for interpretation or not speak, but if the facilitator has this gift of interpretation, he or she should be ready to offer the interpretation.

Mistakes and failures do happen in small group ministry—just like in every other aspect of life. Yet without the liberty to experiment, there is the danger of putting out the Spirit's fire. While all practices of spiritual gifts must be guided by God's inerrant Word, let's remember that they *should* be practiced.

Healing

God wants us all to pray for the sick, but the Holy Spirit has blessed certain members of His Body to pray for healing and see results (see Mark 2:1–12; 8:22–26; 16:17–18; John 9:1–12; 14:12–14; Acts 3:1–8; 14:8–15; 28:8–9; 1 Corinthians 12:9, 28–30; James 5:14–15). God is the only one who can heal, but He often chooses to move through human vessels. Paul uses the term *gifts* of healing, most likely referring to healing in the emotional and spiritual realms, as well as physical healing.

CNN recently aired a TV documentary on the growing popularity of voodoo in the United States. Voodoo gatherings and literature are on the rise in North America. The program highlighted the search for healing of a Caucasian woman who was ridden with cancer. After overcoming many personal inhibitions, she began attending voodoo séances in order to free herself from her disease. CNN not only explained her experience, but it also gave testimonies of "supernatural healing" that have taken place through voodoo. The documentary helped to generate excitement over this growing phenomenon, but voodoo is only one of the many sects that have begun to promote healing to the American masses. New Age philosophy, Eastern religions and various forms of witchcraft offer similar healing remedies.

Jesus, the God-Man, needs to be rediscovered among the pre-Christian power seekers today. He came to this earth bearing a clear message of God's healing power and the Good News of salvation. The all-powerful Ruler of the universe wants to extend His healing hand today.

The small group is the perfect place to pray for those who are suffering from physical, emotional and spiritual conditions. The group is small enough to share needs without intimidation, and because all human beings will eventually face physical and emotional ailments, the time will inevitably come when people will need prayer. If the Holy Spirit has gifted the facilitator or another group member with the gift of healing, allow him or her to pray for the sick person. Jesus will receive glory when the person receives healing. Even if the Holy Spirit grants this gift to someone in the group because the situation demands it, great things will still take place, and again God will receive the glory.

On December 9, 2002, John suffered a stroke, which left his face deformed and the right side of his mouth completely twisted. When the members of his small group learned what had happened, they immediately visited him in the hospital and prayed fervently that God would heal him. As they prayed, John's mouth was instantly healed—right in front of them. This demonstration of God's power encouraged John to dedicate himself to the Lord's service, and many people were encouraged to follow Jesus because of the healing John received.

The small group members responded to John's needs and took it upon themselves to continue to pray for his healing, following the advice of James 5:16: "Confess your sins to each other and pray for each other so that you may be healed." According to James, praying for the sick is a "one-another ministry." Rather than relying on the prayers of an anointed "miracle worker," Christians are instructed to pray for one another. The context of the book of James, moreover, was written to a first-century house-church meeting—not a massive miracle service in a large auditorium.

Whether or not the Holy Spirit gives the gift of healing, we still need to pray for one another. The healing process starts in the group when the leader asks members to share their afflictions and physical needs. Afterward, the leader might ask all group members to stretch out their hands toward the afflicted person while the leader prays a healing prayer. Another option is to ask those near the person to lay their own hands on him or her while the leader prays for God's miraculous touch. Some leaders might ask all group members to gather around the sick person while two or three others pray for physical healing. It is best to conclude each prayer for healing "in Jesus' name," because Jesus said in John 14:13–14: "And I will do whatever you ask in my name, so that the Son may bring glory to the Father. You may ask me for anything in my name, and I will do it."

The phrase "variety is the spice of life" applies well to small group ministry. Small group leaders are wise to vary their prayer methods, especially with regard to prayers for healing. One week, the leader might personally lay hands on the sick while everyone else extends their hands. Another week, the leader might ask various members to pray over the sick person. The key is to not get stuck doing one thing to the exclusion of something else. We all need variety, we need to find new outlets for our energies. But we must always remember that the way to receive God's healing is through confession of our needs.

Allow the Spirit to do what He wants to do. Make Him the center of your discussion. Ask Him to fill you with His grace. Yes, He will come through. He will make Himself known.

Miracles

The gift of miracles is the Spirit-given endowment to believe God for mighty acts that are contrary to the laws of nature and that glorify God (see Exodus 14:21–31; 1 Kings 18:21–40; Matthew 14:25–33; 24:23–24; Luke 10:17–20; John 14:2–14; Acts 9:36–42; 19:11; 20:9–12; Romans 15:18–19; 1 Corinthians 12:10, 28; 2 Corinthians 12:12). The word *miracles* comes from the Greek word *dunamis*, from which we also get our English word *dynamite*. It refers to a work that cannot be produced by natural means. While on earth, Jesus wanted people to know of God's amazing power to work miracles. Approximately thirty percent of the verses in Mark's gospel deal with Jesus' miracle-working power.

My grandmother Martha Nelson was the first one in my immediate family to receive Jesus, and she did so at the age of 74. After being converted from Christian Science into a personal relationship with Jesus Christ, she began attending Kathryn Kuhlman conferences in

Los Angeles. These meetings gave her a firsthand appreciation for the supernatural power of God working through miracles and healing. Her faith in a miraculous God had a major impact on my immediate family, and most especially on my own life.

When God's power is demonstrated through healing, God receives the glory, people are emboldened to tell the Good News to their friends and Christ's Kingdom is extended.

Jesus Christ is the same yesterday, today and forever. He is able to do the same miracles today that He did back when He walked on this earth. Jesus said, in fact, that those who believe in His name will even do greater miracles than He did (see John 14:12).

Discernment of Spirits

The gift of discernment of spirits enables Christians to distinguish between truth and error, and to know with certainty when a behavior has satanic, human or divine origin (see Matthew 16:22–23; Acts 5:1–10; 8:18–24; 13:6–12; 16:16–18; 1 Corinthians 12:10; 1 Thessalonians 5:19–22; 1 John 4:1–6). All believers are able to distinguish truth from error to a certain extent (see Hebrews 5:12–14), but those with the gift of discernment are endowed with the special ability to know with certainty what is true and what is false. The clearest biblical example of the demonstration of this gift occurred when the apostle Peter discerned that Satan had inspired Ananias to lie to the Holy Spirit. Ananias was immediately struck dead, and his wife was as well because she partook in the lie (see Acts 5:1–10).

Even if the facilitator of a small group does not have this particular gift, when a difficult situation takes place in the small group, the facilitator should ask the Holy Spirit for the gift of discernment. The Holy Spirit offers some gifts according to the needs and situation and so, by all means, ask for it if you need it. When a member already has this gift, encourage him or her to speak one-on-one with the person for whom discernment is needed to verify the details. Afterward, if necessary, the member can talk directly to the small group leader.

A small group leader can avoid many problems if he or she just remembers the principle of edification and love. The Holy Spirit freely offers the gifts to the Church to *edify*, not to *destroy* or *tear down*. Remember that the Holy Spirit inspired Paul to write the love chapter and set it squarely in the midst of the chapters concerning spiritual gifts. And immediately after writing about the gifts, Paul continued this theme to the Roman believers: "Be devoted to one another in brotherly love. Honor one another above yourselves" (Romans 12:10). The Holy Spirit is certainly willing to enliven small group ministry through the gifts of the Spirit, but love must dominate all that is said and done.

9

PRAYER THROUGH SMALL GROUPS

As we sat in the prayer room on Saturday night, I felt as if I could touch heaven. Six other pastors and I were at Cypress Creek Church in Wimberley, Texas, surrounded by seven prayer warriors. We were sitting in the middle, and they formed a half-circle around us. With pencil and paper in hand, these intercessors wrote down what God was showing them in preparation of their prayer for us.

The prayer warriors asked each of us to share our particular needs and prayer requests. They asked questions in order to make sure they knew how to pray specifically. And then the prayer time began. These warriors intermingled Scripture and prophecy in their prayers over us. The atmosphere was filled with God's presence, and I practically floated away.

I have taken two groups of pastors to Cypress Creek Church. Both times, I came away energized by the power of God through prayer. When this church was first started in 1994, the first person they hired was Cecilia Belvin, the pastor of prayer.

Cecilia has the gift of intercession, and as she began to develop this ministry, other like-minded prayer warriors joined with her. Today, Cypress Creek Church has one of the most vital prayer ministries I have ever encountered. God has blessed this church abundantly because they have placed Him first.

Even though the gift of prayer is not explicitly taught in Scripture as a spiritual gift, it seems evident that some people have been given this gift. The gift of prayer enables Christians to pray for concrete requests over a long period of time. As Peter Wagner says, "Certain Christians, it seems to me, have a special ability to pray for an extended period of time on a regular basis and see frequent and specific answers to their prayers."[1]

I include this gift of prayer in the last chapter because I believe that prayer should characterize Spirit-led groups—whether people in these groups have the gift of prayer or not. If a person in a small group has the gift of prayer, intercession will flow naturally. For the rest of us, it will require hard work.

Intercession for Evangelism

Small group-evangelism techniques abound. In previous books, I have written about small group picnics, barbeques, videos in the small group, praying over an empty chair and other evangelistic methods. I have a growing conviction, however, that the strategy of prayer is so much more effective that it causes all the other strategies to pale in comparison. Sustained intercessory prayer is the "nuclear" arsenal in the Christian's evangelistic armament.

When God's people pray fervently and wholeheartedly, God Himself releases supernatural power, and miracles take place. One leader said,

> The place I was staying was rife with witchcraft and poverty. I initiated prayer action within my cell, which grew to . . . five cells. When the powers in the air are broken, the light of God shines magnificently, bringing healing and redemption to all the hurting and destitute.[2]

Effective groups and leaders are dedicated to prayer. They recognize that the most effective tool to win non-Christians is fervent prayer. They also understand that they are involved in a spiritual battle, and that no one will be won to Jesus Christ apart from the supernatural intervention of the Holy Spirit. He is the one who gives victory and heals hearts. Only Jesus can set the captives free and make a person whole.

Effective small groups reach out through prayer. As Jesus instructed, they first bind the strong man, and then they go in and spoil the goods (see Matthew 12:29).

Justin and Lucy moved into an apartment complex with the priority of starting a small group. When my wife asked Justin if he had made any contacts with the neighbors, knowing he was planning on doing so, he replied, "I'm not ready to start reaching out to them quite yet because I have not bathed them with prayer sufficiently." Justin takes prayer warfare seriously. He knows that the Holy Spirit must first open hearts before they can respond to the truth of the Gospel.

Those who do not know Christ are blinded by demonic forces that do not want them to see the Good News of Jesus Christ. Paul wrote about this reality:

> And even if our gospel is veiled, it is veiled to those who are perishing. The god of this age has blinded the minds of unbelievers, so that they cannot see the light of the gospel of the glory of Christ, who is the image of God.
>
> 2 Corinthians 4:3–4

Prayer comes first; outreach second. God's work is always more effective than our own human effort, because it assures long-term success. From my years of ministry experience, I have noticed that it is one thing to repeat the "sinner's prayer" with someone and claim a conversion, but it is quite another matter to see the person regenerated. Many of my own converts were just that—my own converts. In other words, they were never truly converted. When God converts someone, the person is a true convert.

A Spirit-filled group prioritizes prayer. Prayer is the life-breath and atmosphere of effective groups. Intercession prepares the ground for nonbelievers to receive Christ. Intercessory prayer is spiritual warfare and demands battle-like persistence in order to conquer enemy strongholds. But rest assured, Satan will not relinquish control without a battle. Encourage your small group to pray. Esteem those who take prayer seriously, and hold them up as examples to the rest of the group.

In my own small group, Shaun shared this: "Please pray for my eighteen-year-old son, Jeremy. He received Jesus as a boy, but now he's taking drugs, he's in and out of jail and he's on the verge of suicide." As a cell group, we committed ourselves to pray for Jeremy every day. During the Thursday morning prayer meeting, I sensed a relief in my spirit as I prayed for Jeremy, as if something was about to happen.

The next day, Jeremy's mom, Gina, called, saying that "out of nowhere" Jeremy mentioned his need to get right with God. We invited Jeremy to our church camp the following Saturday night, and he came with his girlfriend. God moved in Jeremy's life, and the following week after camp, Jeremy starting attending a Bible study—for the first time in seven years.

The best way to mobilize the entire group to intercede for nonbelievers is by asking each member to write down the names of friends, relatives or other contacts, with the purpose of praying for their salvation. It is a great idea to then write the names of each member on a large poster and ask the entire group to pray in unison for the names on the poster. Faith Community Baptist Church's training manual exhorts potential cell leaders to "make mention of your unbeliever friends in the cell meetings. Encourage all the cell members to pray for them daily. God will answer these prayers."[3]

It should be commended when a small group can lift their eyes beyond their own neighborhood to the unreached people of the world. God is pleased when a group practices warfare prayer for the non-Christian masses of the world, especially those living in the "10/40 window"—the geographical rectangle between 10 degrees and 40 degrees north latitude, in which 90 percent of unreached people groups live.

I visited one church that asked each of its small groups to conclude with intercessory prayer for the unreached peoples of the world. To that end, they have developed an excellent series of prayer profiles on unreached groups for other churches and cell groups to use.

Intercession for New Leaders

Along with praying for non-Christian friends, a small group should also pray for those who will start a new group. Avoid prayers of doubt, such as: "Lord, if it be Your will to multiply this cell group . . ." The faithful cell member prays believing that multiplication *is* God's will (see 2 Peter 3:9–10; 1 Timothy 2:4–5).

Scott Kellar began to lead his group in Escondido, California, in 2000, and he has been leading a cell group ever since. He has multiplied his cell group four times, and he personally cares for the leaders he has developed. Scott believes that the key to his success is his fervent prayer for each member in the group.

Scott began to pray for Melissa, one of the group members. After praying for her for two months, he approached Melissa about the possibility of one day leading her own group. She flatly refused with the words, "I'm not ready." But Scott continued to pray for her, asking God to open her heart. He waited for six more months and then approached her with the same question about group leadership. "Sure," she replied. Now Melissa is successfully leading her own group, and Scott continues to coach her and her husband. Scott continually lifts up Melissa in prayer, knowing that the devil would like to attack her ministry.

Floyd L. Schwanz addresses the topic of "How to Birth New Groups" in his book, *Growing Small Groups*, counseling cell leaders to "get their group pregnant." How can they do this? Through prayer. He advises cell leaders to include a prayer in each week's meeting for those who will help start a new group, saying, "It gives the Holy Spirit an additional opportunity to work with the hearts of potential leaders."[4]

Intercession and Fasting

Carl Everett, director of Bethany Cell Church Network, started out by leading a cell group. As his group multiplied several times, each daughter cell grew and prospered. Carl boils down the secret to his success into three words: "Prayer, prayer, prayer."

Cell preparation for Carl and his wife, Gaynel, includes fasting and prayer on the day of the cell meeting. Before the meeting, they anoint the food, the sidewalks, the yard, every room in the house and even each seat to be used that night. Carl prays for the members and for God's anointing on his own life. They wait until after the meeting (during the refreshment time) before eating, choosing to fast and pray that God's will be accomplished in the hearts of the people.

The Everetts' example is not unusual at Bethany, where leaders are encouraged to fast and pray before group meetings. Some fast the whole day, others until 3 P.M., while others may skip just one meal. Carl says, "It is important to mobilize as many from the group as possible to fast and pray."

Fasting and prayer are a dual threat to the enemy. The devil leaves when we pray, but he flees when we fast and pray. When fasting, the believer enters a new level of commitment and dedication—a dedication that involves laying aside personal pleasure and enjoyment.

169

Omar Cabrero is the founder of the Church of the Future in Buenos Aires, Argentina. His small group-based church is one of the largest in Argentina, with approximately 150,000 members in 188 churches.[5] Omar discovered that the best way for his church to evangelize people was to rent a hotel room in a city for the purpose of fasting and prayer. For days, he would engage in spiritual warfare for the people of that city until he felt they were released from Satan's grip. When he sensed that God's work had been accomplished, he would then begin an evangelistic campaign, in which thousands upon thousands would receive Jesus as Savior and Lord.

When we fast, we enter the presence of the living God in a more in-depth and personal way. Fasting helps us to hear God's voice because we become more sensitive to Him. It clears out the cobwebs in our minds and helps us to see with spiritual eyes. It also provides additional power to intercede for those who need it most.

Creative Intercessory Prayer

Effective small group facilitators seek to place prayer at the center of group life, knowing that prayer cannot be overemphasized. Some great ideas to jumpstart cells for prayer include the following:

- Break into groups of two or three. This allows more people to enter into prayer and is less intimidating for quieter members.
- Ask individual cell members to intercede, calling on them by name.

- Train your group to pray short, conversational prayers that provide greater interaction and agreement. This allows more people to pray and helps prevent one person from dominating the prayer time.

- During the last fifteen minutes of the group meeting, ask the men to go into one room to pray and the women to pray in another room. Often there is more liberty to share prayer requests among gender-specific groups.

- Try using "concert prayer." C. Peter Wagner describes this as having "all those present in the prayer meeting pray out loud at the same time."[6] Korean Christians have popularized this style of prayer. In David Cho's church, the leader gives the signal to begin, and a roar of prayer floods the church until a bell signals that it is time to quit.

Cells are simply the conduit of the Holy Spirit; they are not an end in themselves. Prayer empowers cells and makes them a blessing to others.

Prayer Walking

Prayer walking as a group is precursory work to prepare the ground for harvest. It is also a public proclamation to the forces of darkness that God rules and wants to awaken souls bound in darkness. When a group walks around a neighborhood, it is reminiscent of the Israelites walking around the walls of Jericho. It might appear foolish to others, but it is a tribute to the power of God to work in people's lives. It proclaims the victory of Christ over evil spirits and over the demonic hordes that would seek to destroy and ransack that particular area.

God said to Joshua before the conquest of Canaan, "I will give you every place where you set your foot, as I promised Moses" (Joshua 1:3). The problem for the Israelites, as it is for us, is that there are giants in the land, giants that do not move easily, especially in Western culture.

Western rationalism and materialistic pleasure have grounded many people in their homes, watching television for hours upon hours. They will not move easily to attend your group meeting—unless God rolls away the stone. So many people, often unwittingly, have succumbed to the gods of personal pleasure and affluence. It is my conviction that only prayer will overcome this malady. Only God can change a person's propensity for materialistic greed.

As a small group goes out into a neighborhood, it is proclaiming that God is the One who must remove the giants in the land. The group is declaring their dependence on Him.

Begin with a Plan

Planning is essential for prayer walking. If possible, give the group a couple weeks of advance notice. They will need to prepare themselves both physically (such as securing the appropriate clothing) and spiritually.

Often when the group engages in prayer walking, the lesson time will be shorter, so the meeting can still last about one-and-a-half hours, with the prayer walk included. I recommend having a lesson on prayer, spiritual warfare or some other aspect of the Spirit's work in preparation for prayer walking. I also encourage everyone to go out to pray, although some might insist on staying behind and praying while others go.

If there are more than fifteen adults, divide into two groups. I encourage children to also come on the prayer walk, but they must understand that the goal is prayer, not play.

Act Normal

Most of the time, those in the neighborhood should not know what the group is doing. Everyone should have his or her eyes open and be talking, not shouting, so that it appears as though a group is simply walking, talking and having a good time.

It is always good when the host or facilitator gives a running commentary of the different neighbors for the purpose of prayer. The host might say, for example, "Tim and Susan live here, and they've recently been going through some marriage problems. Pray for God to mend their hearts" or "The Thompsons are born-again believers and go to the local Baptist church; let's pray for God's blessing on their lives."

If the group is small, it is a good idea to allow anyone to pray at any time, although the facilitator or core team member should generally guide the prayer walk. If the group is large, it is best to ask each person by name to pray for a particular house, such as: "Jane, would you please pray for Tim and Susan?"

Be Sensitive to the Spirit

During certain seasons of the year, more people will be outside, and prayer walking can provide a great opportunity to greet people. My own group uses prayer walking as an effective way not only to pray for the neighborhood but also to communicate with those around our house. God has given us various opportunities to share our faith and reach out to people around us.

During our prayer walks, when we see people outside, we greet them in a friendly, loving way. Sometimes one of the members feels led to speak about Christ and invite the person to our cell. It is not necessary, however, to share Christ with each person. Often a friendly wave, a warm greeting or engaging in small talk is part of the preparatory ministry for future conversations.

Divine Desperation

God is raising up an army of Spirit-filled small groups. The world's largest church in the history of Christianity can teach us about intercessory prayer. When I visited Pastor Cho's Yoido Full Gospel Church in April 1997, I estimated that there were 253,000 people attending the mother church, along with an additional 25,000 cell groups. Someone had told me before going to Korea that the church was in decline. But when I was there, I thought to myself, *If this is decline, what does church growth look like?!*

It was not until the next morning that I understood the secret of the success of this great church. It was snowing lightly that Monday morning in April. I bundled up and went down to the main sanctuary at 5:30 A.M. There, I saw three thousand Korean saints on their knees crying out to God: "Give us Korea for Your Son, Jesus, dear Lord." I realized that the largest church in the history of Christianity was a praying church. This church was willing to pay the price in prayer, and God was blessing them mightily as a result.

That same Monday morning, I took a bus to Prayer Mountain, a former cemetery that has been converted into a mountain of prayer. An estimated ten thousand people pass through this prayer mountain every week. The Yoido Full Gospel Church has carved hundreds of caves into the side of this mountain for the purpose of prayer. It was exciting to walk by the prayer caves and hear the cries of God's people ascending to the throne of God. These Korean believers reminded me of Epaphras, a person whom Paul said "is always wrestling in prayer for you, that you may stand firm in all the will of God, mature and fully assured" (Colossians 4:12). The verb *wrestle* in this verse literally means "to agonize." *This is what I need,* I said to myself. *I lack fervency. I need to wrestle more with God in prayer.* Compared to the Korean Christians, my prayer life was halfhearted at best. I left Korea inspired to bolster the fervency of my own prayer life.

Until cell leadership is convinced that only God can convert a non-Christian and raise up new leaders, little will happen. Trite moments of prayer in a cell group are incapable of breaking the spirit of lethargy. Before prayer can make a difference in the cell, the cell leadership must "know that they know" that unless God breathes His life into our methodologies, they are just wood, hay and stubble. When Jesus saw the pressing needs of the multitude, He did not tell the disciples to initiate the latest evangelism-training program. Rather, He commanded them to "ask the Lord of the harvest . . . to send out workers into his harvest field" (Matthew 9:38).

Intercessory prayer is hard work, and it requires persistence. Yet the fruit of it is renewed members and salvation for the lost. At times you will want to give up. Don't. God is hearing your prayers and is pleased with them. In His time, the answer will come—quickly.

The Spirit-Filled Small Group

All those reading this book will agree that we need more of God's Spirit in our small groups. All of us can also agree that the Spirit must control both small group leaders and members. Walking in the Spirit and receiving His fullness is an essential part of the Christian life. Most of us, in addition, would agree that the spiritual gifts are for today and need to be practiced. Some might be more hesitant than others to allow certain gifts (such as revelatory prophecy) to function in their small groups.

The main question, however, is not what we agree or disagree on. The main question is, How can we have more of Him today in the 21st century? The Holy Spirit yearns to flow among yielded vessels. I believe the Spirit is just as willing to fill leaders and groups today as He was back in the days of the apostle Paul. Most likely you believe the same.

Allow Him to fill you and your group so that you can effectively penetrate your neighborhood, city and world for Jesus Christ. As the gifts of the Spirit flow freely in your small group, Jesus will be glorified and His Church will taste a little bit of the heavenly delight that will one day be ours throughout eternity.

NOTES

Introduction

1. George Barna, "Protestants, Catholics and Mormons Reflect Diverse Levels of Religious Activity," http://www.barna.org/cgi-bin/PagePressRelease .asp?PressReleaseID=93&Reference=F (4 October 2001).

2. Lawrence Khong, *The Apostolic Cell Church: Practical Strategies for Growth and Outreach from the Story of Faith Community Baptist Church* (Singapore: Touch Ministries International, 2000), 33.

3. In my book *Cell Church Solutions* (Moreno Valley, Calif.: CCS Publishing, 2005), I lay out 44 case-study churches from 17 denominations and church networks, which include Assemblies of God, American Baptist, Calvary Chapel, Church of Christ, Church of God, Christian and Missionary Alliance, Covenant, Dove Christian Fellowship, Free Methodist, Lutheran, Nazarene, Southern Baptist, Pentecostal, Pentecostal Free Will Baptist, United Methodist, Vineyard and Wesleyan. Some of these churches are charismatic and others are not. These cell churches are located in 18 U.S. states and two provinces of Canada. The variety of these churches argues against saying that only Pentecostal or charismatic churches make great cell churches.

4. Most books on Christian leadership agree that leadership is influence. Dr. Robert J. Clinton defines leadership this way: "A leader, as defined from a study of biblical leadership . . . is a person with God-given capacity and with God-given responsibility who is influencing a specific group of God's people toward God's purposes for the group" [*Leadership Perspectives* (Altadena, Calif.: Barnabas Publishers, 1993), 14]. C. Peter Wagner uses the idea of influencing a group of people toward God's purpose to define the "gift of leadership" in the New Testament (see Romans 12:8). He says: "The gift of leadership is the special ability that God gives to certain members of the Body of Christ to set goals in accordance with God's purpose for the future and to communicate these goals to others in such a way that

they voluntarily and harmoniously work together to accomplish those goals for the glory of God" [*Your Spiritual Gifts Can Help Your Church Grow* (Ventura, Calif.: Regal, 1979), 162]. The Touch Outreach Seminar for zone supervisors describes a leader as ". . . a person who *encourages* others, who *motivates* others to meet the group goals. . . ." [*Zone Supervisor Seminar* (Houston, Tex.: Touch Outreach Ministries, 1997), F-1]. In this book, I will follow the above consensus that a leader is one who influences a particular group to meet its goal.

5. Clinton, 14.

6. In my book *Leadership Explosion* (Houston, Tex.: Touch Publications, 2001), I talk about receiving training and discipleship in preparation to lead a cell group.

7. I consider C. Peter Wagner's book *Your Spiritual Gifts Can Help Your Church Grow* to be the best book on spiritual gifts available today. The second best book, in my opinion, is *The 3 Colors of Ministry* by Christian A. Schwarz (St. Charles, Ill.: ChurchSmart Resources, 2001).

8. My books *Reap the Harvest* (Houston, Tex.: Touch Publications, 1999) and *Cell Church Solutions* (Moreno Valley, Calif.: CCS Publishing, 2005) talk about the senior pastor's role in the small group-driven church.

9. Other small group ministry topics that I have addressed elsewhere include:

- Leading a cell group: *How to Lead a Great Cell Group Meeting* (Touch Publications, 2001)
- How to multiply the cell group: *Home Cell Group Explosion* (Touch Publications, 1998)
- How to prepare spiritually for cell ministry: *An Appointment with the King* (Chosen, 2002)
- How to practically organize your cell system: *Reap the Harvest* (Touch Publications, 1999); *Cell Church Explosion* (Editorial Clie, 2005)
- How to train future cell leaders: *Leadership Explosion* (Touch Publications, 2001)
- How to coach and care for cell leaders: *How to Be a Great Cell Group Coach* (Cell Group Resources, 2003); *Groups of Twelve* (Touch Publications, 2000); *From Twelve to Three* (Touch Publications, 2002)
- How to fine-tune your cell system: *Making Cell Groups Work Navigation Guide* (Cell Group Resources, 2003)
- Principles from the second-largest church in the world: *Passion and Persistence* (Cell Group Resources, 2004)

For more information on these materials, visit our website, www.cellchurch solutions.com, or call 1-888-511-9995.

Chapter 1: The Filling of the Spirit

1. The Holy Spirit is called God (see Acts 5:3–4; 1 Corinthians 2:11; 2 Corinthians 3:17) and He possesses divine attributes, such as omniscience (see 1 Corinthians 2:10–11), omnipresence (see Psalm 139:7) and omnipotence (see

Zechariah 4:6). He is the third Person of the Trinity (see Matthew 28:19). For more on this topic, see René Pache, *The Person and Work of the Holy Spirit* (Chicago, Ill.: Moody, 1954), 14–19.

2. See 1 Corinthians 2:10 (searching), Romans 8:26 (helping) and John 14:26 (teaching).

3. See 1 Corinthians 2:11 (knowledge), 1 Corinthians 12:11 (will), Romans 8:27 (mind), Romans 15:30 (love), Nehemiah 9:20 (instruction) and Ephesians 4:30 (grief).

4. Craig Keener, *Gift Giver: The Holy Spirit for Today* (Grand Rapids, Mich.: Baker Academic, 2001), 147–48.

5. See *An Appointment with the King* (Grand Rapids, Mich.: Chosen, 2002).

6. Jim Egli's Ph.D. from Regent University (completed in 2003) involved surveying small group-based churches to determine factors in their growth or decline. In October 2003, Egli shared these observations at the Touch Field Forum in Houston, Texas.

Chapter 2: Living in the Spirit

1. Mikel Neumann, *Home Groups for Urban Cultures* (Pasadena, Calif.: William Carey Library, 1999), 82.

2. Everett Lewis Cattell, *The Spirit of Holiness* (Kansas City, Mo.: Beacon Hill, 1963), 54–55.

3. Matthew Henry, in *Matthew Henry's Commentary on the Bible* (Peabody, Mass.: Hendrickson Publishers, 1991) on CD-ROM, writes, "We may be present in spirit with those churches and Christians from whom we are absent in body; for the communion of saints is a spiritual thing. Paul had heard concerning the Colossians that they were orderly and regular; and though he had never seen them, nor was present with them, he tells them he could easily think himself among them, and look with pleasure upon their good behavior."

4. For complete information on factors that affect and do not affect small group multiplication, see my book *Home Cell Group Explosion* (Houston, Tex.: Touch Publications, 1998).

Chapter 3: Worship and the Word in Spirit-Filled Groups

1. David Hocking, *The Seven Laws of Christian Leadership* (Ventura, Calif.: Regal, 1991), 63.

Chapter 4: Edification in Spirit-Filled Groups

1. George Barna, as quoted in Julie Gorman, *Community That Is Christian* (Wheaton, Ill.: Victor Books, 1993), 81.

2. Larry Crabb, *Connecting* (Nashville, Tenn.: Word Publishing, 1997), 31.

Chapter 5: Christ's Body and Small Groups

1. James H. Rutz, *The Open Church* (Auburn, Maine: The SeedSowers, 1992), 47.

2. John Mallison, *Growing Christians in Small Groups* (London: Scripture Union, 1989), 5.

3. Elton Trueblood, as quoted in Edward F. Murphy, *The Gifts of the Spirit and the Mission of the Church* (Pasadena, Calif.: Fuller Theological Seminary, 1972), 152.

4. Paul [David] Yonggi Cho, *Successful Home Cell Groups* (Plainfield, N.J.: Logos International, 1981), 50–52.

5. Bill Easum, "Emerging Trends for Effective Ministry in the 21st Century," *Journal for the American Society for Church Growth* (Spring 2001): 45.

6. The International Charismatic Mission in Bogota, Columbia (probably the fourth-largest church in the world), and the Elim Church in San Salvador (perhaps the second- or third-largest church in the world) are in this category. These two churches are the largest cell-based churches in Latin America. The senior pastor of the Elim Church, Mario Vega, told me that prophecy, tongues and interpretation can be exercised in the small group, but they ask for a pastor to be present in such cases.

Chapter 6: How the Gifts Work in Small Groups

1. Various other Greek words are used in 1 Corinthians 12:1–7 to describe the Spirit's working through gifts:

verse 1: *pneumatikon*—spiritual endowments, rather than natural talents and gifts

verse 4: *charismata*—free gifts of God's goodness, rather than earned or merited

verse 5: *diakonian*—function or ministry in the Church, opportunities to serve others

verse 6: *energematon*—workings that are momentary, for a particular purpose, rather than a permanent possession

verse 7: *phanerosis*—active exhibition or manifestation of God's power, reflecting His power and glory

2. Ray C. Stedman, *Body Life* (Glendale, Calif.: Regal, 1972), 66–77; C. Peter Wagner, *Your Spiritual Gifts Can Help Your Church Grow* (Ventura, Calif.: Regal Books, 1979), 9; Robert J. Clinton, *Spiritual Gifts* (Coral Gables, Fla.: West Indies Mission, 1975), 40, 100; Rick Yohn, *Discover Your Spiritual Gift and Use It* (Wheaton, Ill.: Tyndale House, 1983), 128–30; John Wimber, *Healing Ministry and Church Growth* (Pasadena, Calif.: Fuller Theological Seminary, 1983), 40.

3. The general categories were taken from Paul Ford, *Unleash Your Church* (Pasadena, Calif.: Charles E. Fuller Institute, 1993), 55, although I altered the order and made several changes.

4. Both Christian A. Schwarz in *The 3 Colors of Ministry* (St. Charles, Ill.: ChurchSmart Resources, 2001), 157, and Wagner, 272, go into detail on these additional gifts.

5. My book *Home Cell Group Explosion* (Houston, Tex.: Touch Publications, 1998) goes into detail about the results of my Ph.D. study.

6. Richard B. Gaffin Jr., as quoted in Wayne A. Grudem, ed., *Are Miraculous Gifts for Today?* (Grand Rapids, Mich.: Zondervan, 1996), 62.

7. John Wimber, as quoted in Steven W. and Victoria L. Long, *The Word of Knowledge: A Historical, Biblical, and Applicational Study* (Pasadena, Calif.: Fuller Theological Seminary, 1989), 187.

8. John Wimber's classroom teaching and powerpoints during his Signs and Wonders course at Fuller Theological Seminary, as quoted by John F. Maher Jr., As the Spirit Wills: Leadership and Administration in the Local Church for the Manifestation of All the Gifts of the Spirit (Pasadena, Calif.: Fuller Theological Seminary, 1992), 86.

9. Various gift surveys include: Dr. Mel Carbonell's gift survey that features a gift inventory and the DISC personality evaluation (see www.uniquelyyou.com); Alvin J. VanderGriend's gift survey (Christian Reformed Church, CRC Publications); Paul Ford's gift survey (ChurchSmart Resources); Christian Schwarz's gift survey (ChurchSmart Resources).

10. Robert L. Saucy, as quoted in Grudem, 141.

11. Greg Ogden, as quoted in Ford, 49.

Chapter 7: Service and Equipping Gifts

1. Anyone wanting to read a thorough exposition of the four different positions on the controversy surrounding the gifts of the Spirit should read Wayne A. Grudem, ed., *Are Miraculous Gifts for Today?* This is an excellent introductory book and represents each view on the topic fairly.

2. Schwarz, 120.

3. Ron Nichols, *Good Things Come in Small Groups* (Downers Grove, Ill.: InterVarsity, 1985), 25.

4. George Mueller, as quoted in John Packo, *Find and Use Your Spiritual Gift* (Harrisburg, Pa.: Christian Publications, 1980), 52.

5. Packo, 64.

6. Since the early 1980s, Peter Wagner and David Cho have declared that ten percent of believers have this gift. David Cho has stated that only those with the gift of evangelism could lead a cell to the point of multiplication. My research of seven hundred small group leaders, however, showed that the gift of evangelism *did not* correlate with a leader's ability to multiply a small group, because small group leaders harness the giftedness of everyone in the group. It is significant that the research of Christian A. Schwarz in *The 3 Colors of Ministry* (116) confirms that only ten percent have the gift of evangelism.

Chapter 8: The Worship Gifts

1. Sally Morgenthaler, *Worship Evangelism* (Grand Rapids, Mich.: Zondervan, 1999).
2. W. E. Vine and F. F. Bruce, *Vine's Expository Dictionary of Old and New Testament Words* (Old Tappan, N.J.: Revell, 1981). Vine defines the word PROPHĒTEIA προφητεἴα (4394) to signify the speaking forth of the mind and counsel of God: *pro*, forth, phēmi, to speak. See "prophet." In the New Testament it is used (*a*) of the gift, e.g., Romans 12:6; 1 Corinthians 12:10; 13:2; (*b*) either of the exercise of the gift or of that which is prophesied, e.g., Matthew 13:14; 1 Corinthians 13:8; 14:6, 22 and 1 Thessalonians 5:20, "prophesying(s)"; 1 Timothy 1:18; 4:14; 2 Peter 1:20, 21; Revelation 1:3; 11:6; 19:10; 22:7, 10, 18, 19. Vine says: "Though much of O.T. prophecy was purely predictive, see Micah 5:2, e.g., and cp. John 11:51, prophecy is not necessarily, nor even primarily, fore-telling. It is the declaration of that which cannot be known by natural means, Matthew 26:68, it is the forth-telling of the will of God, whether with reference to the past, the present or the future, see Genesis 20:7; Deuteronomy 18:18; Revelation 10:11; 11:3."
3. Ralph Neighbour, audiotape. *From Structures to the Incarnation of Christ*, 2003. Presented in Houston and accessed online at http://www.touchusa.org/avtraining.asp.
4. Keener, 120.
5. Wagner, 230.
6. Pat Robertson, as quoted in Long, 111.
7. John Bevere, *Thus Saith the Lord? How to Know When God Is Speaking to You through Another* (Lake Mary, Fla.: Creation House, 1999) 85–94.
8. Keener, 174.

Chapter 9: Prayer through Small Groups

1. Wagner, 75.
2. Personal e-mail received on 12/11/2002 from Godfrey Kahangi, who went from cell leader to coach to pastor at Kampala Pentecostal Church in Kampala, Uganda. The senior pastor is Gary Skinner.
3. Cell Leader Intern Training (Singapore: Touch Ministries International, 1996), Section 5, 4.
4. Floyd L. Schwanz, *Growing Small Groups* (Kansas City, Mo.: Beacon Hill Press, 1995), 140.
5. Information obtained from Miguel Robles, a well-respected pastor in Buenos Aires, who researched the church.
6. C. Peter Wagner, *Churches That Pray* (Ventura, Calif.: Regal, 1993), 119.

BIBLIOGRAPHY

Bevere, John. *Thus Saith the Lord? How to Know When God Is Speaking to You through Another.* Lake Mary, Fla.: Creation House, 1999.

Cattell, Everett Lewis. *The Spirit of Holiness.* Kansas City, Mo.: Beacon Hill, 1963.

Cho, Paul [David] Yonggi. *Successful Home Cell Groups.* Plainfield, N.J.: Logos International, 1981.

Clinton, Robert J. *Leadership Perspectives.* Altadena, Calif.: Barnabas Publishers, 1993.

———. *Spiritual Gifts.* Coral Gables, Fla.: West Indies Mission, 1975.

Comiskey, Joel. *An Appointment with the King.* Grand Rapids, Mich.: Chosen, 2002.

———. *Cell Church Solutions.* Moreno Valley, Calif.: CCS Publishing, 2005.

———. *Home Cell Group Explosion.* Houston, Tex.: Touch Publications, 1998.

———. *Leadership Explosion.* Houston, Tex.: Touch Publications, 2001.

———. *Reap the Harvest.* Houston, Tex.: Touch Publications, 1999.

Crabb, Larry. *Connecting.* Nashville, Tenn.: Word Publishing, 1997.

Easum, Bill. "Emerging Trends for Effective Ministry in the 21st Century." *Journal for the American Society for Church Growth* (Spring 2001): 45.

Ford, Paul. *Unleash Your Church.* Pasadena, Calif.: Charles E. Fuller Institute, 1993.

Gorman, Julie. *Community That Is Christian.* Wheaton, Ill.: Victor Books, 1993.

Grudem, William, ed. *Are Miraculous Gifts for Today?* Grand Rapids, Mich.: Zondervan, 1996.

Hocking, David. *The Seven Laws of Christian Leadership.* Ventura, Calif.: Regal, 1991.

Keener, Craig. *Gift Giver: The Holy Spirit for Today.* Grand Rapids, Mich.: Baker Academic, 2001.

Khong, Lawrence. *The Apostolic Cell Church: Practical Strategies for Growth and Outreach from the Story of Faith Community Baptist Church.* Singapore: Touch Ministries International, 2000.

Long, Steven W. and Victoria L. Long. *The Word of Knowledge: A Historical, Biblical, and Applicational Study.* Pasadena, Calif.: Fuller Theological Seminary, 1989.

Maher, John F., Jr. *As the Spirit Wills: Leadership and Administration in the Local Church for the Manifestation of All the Gifts of the Spirit.* Pasadena, Calif.: Fuller Theological Seminary, 1992.

Mallison, John. *Growing Christians in Small Groups.* London: Scripture Union, 1989.

Miller, Basil. *George Mueller: Man of Faith and Miracles.* Minneapolis, Minn.: Dimension Books, 1941.

Morgenthaler, Sally. *Worship Evangelism.* Grand Rapids, Mich.: Zondervan, 1999.

Murphy, Edward F. *The Gifts of the Spirit and the Mission of the Church.* Pasadena, Calif.: Fuller Theological Seminary, 1972.

Nichols, Ron. *Good Things Come in Small Groups.* Downers Grove, Ill.: InterVarsity, 1985.

Neumann, Mikel. *Home Groups for Urban Cultures.* Pasadena, Calif.: William Carey Library, 1999.

Pache, René. *The Person and Work of the Holy Spirit.* Chicago, Ill.: Moody, 1954.

Packo, John. *Find and Use Your Spiritual Gift*. Harrisburg, Pa.: Christian Publications, 1980.

Rutz, James H. *The Open Church*. Auburn, Maine: The Seed-Sowers, 1992.

Schwanz, Floyd L. *Growing Small Groups*. Kansas City, Mo.: Beacon Hill Press, 1995.

Schwarz, Christian A. *The 3 Colors of Ministry*. St. Charles, Ill.: ChurchSmart Resources, 2001.

Stedman, Ray C. *Body Life*. Glendale, Calif.: Regal, 1972.

Wagner, C. Peter. *Your Spiritual Gifts Can Help Your Church Grow*. Ventura, Calif.: Regal, 1979.

———. *Churches That Pray*. Ventura, Calif.: Regal, 1993.

Wimber, John. *Healing Ministry and Church Growth*. Pasadena, Calif.: Fuller Theological Seminary, 1983.

Yohn, Rick. *Discover Your Spiritual Gift and Use It*. Wheaton, Ill.: Tyndale, 1983.

INDEX

Index

Neumann, Mikel, 36
Nichols, Ron, 130
nonbelievers, ministering to, 147

obedience, 13, 60–61
Ogden, Greg, 121
one-another ministry, 158
one-on-one relationships, 79
organization, 127
outreach, 166
outward focus, 50

parable of the talents, 105
participation, 94
pastoring, 111, 139–40
Paul, 28, 34, 103, 104, 116, 133, 135, 152–53
peace, 30, 39–43
Pentecost, 24, 28, 32, 83
Pentecostal churches, 12, 177n3
persecution, 84
Peter, 105
Pioneer 10 satellite, 32
postmodern world, 94
power, and prayer, 25–28
power evangelism, 147
Powers, Ginger, 10
praise, 74–75
prayer, 25–28, 44–46, 55, 111
    methods, 158–59
prayer walking, 171–74
preaching, 92, 145
priesthood of all believers, 91–94
programs, in the church, 90–91
prophecy, 59, 99, 104, 111, 125, 135, 143, 144–45, 180n6
    and nonbelievers, 147–49
    and preaching, 145
prophets, 104, 182n2 (chap. 8)
psalms, 55

quiet time, 29–31

Reformation, 91
rejection, 67
relationships, 117–18
renewal, 72

representation, 94
revelation, 150, 152
revelatory prophecy, 149–53
rhema, 57–58
Robertson, Pat, 150–51

sarcasm, 75
Satan, 31, 41, 76–77, 166
Saucy, Robert L., 118
Schwanz, Floyd L., 168
Schwarz, Christian, 130, 181n6 (chap. 7), 181n9
self-chastisement, 68
selfishness, 44
self-sufficiency, 34
sensationalism, 107
sensitivity, to Spirit, 72–73
service, 103, 110–11, 126–32
sharing, 72, 96
Shekinah Fellowship, 23–24
shepherding, 139
showmanship, 107
shyness, 69
silence, 55, 73–74
sin, 27, 28, 41, 76
singing, 54–55, 72
single-parent households, 67
situational view (reception of gifts), 114–15
Skinner, Gary, 182n2 (chap. 9)
small groups
    flexibility, 129
    size of, 95–98
    and spiritual gifts, 93–94, 117
Smith, Chuck, 23
Solomon, 27
"Spirit-filled," 10
spiritual gifts, 11–12, 16, 42, 52–53, 87–88, 90, 91, 102–3
    categories of, 110–12
    identification of, 117–21
    in large-group contexts, 98–100
    and needs, 148
    number of, 109–10
    and small groups, 93–94
    use of, 104–7
Stedman, Ray, 110
steering, 127

Joel Comiskey holds the Ph.D. from Fuller Theological Seminary and is an internationally recognized cell church consultant. He has served as a missionary with the Christian and Missionary Alliance in Quito, Ecuador, and is now the founding pastor of Wellspring, a small group-based church in Southern California. Joel has written best-selling books on the worldwide cell group movement and teaches as adjunct professor at several theological seminaries.

Joel and his wife, Celyce, have three daughters and live in Moreno Valley, California. For the last nine years the Comiskeys have enjoyed opening their home for small group ministry and are excited to watch their daughters develop their spiritual gifts in the small group setting. Joel enjoys basketball, computers and the outdoors. More information about the Comiskeys can be found at www .comiskey.org or www.joelcomiskeygroup.com.

Resources by Joel Comiskey

Joel Comiskey's previous books cover the following topics

- Leading a cell group (*How to Lead a Great Cell Group Meeting, 2001, 2009*).
- How to multiply the cell group (*Home Cell Group Explosion, 1998*).
- How to prepare spiritually for cell ministry (*An Appointment with the King, 2002*).
- How to practically organize your cell system (*Reap the Harvest,1999; Cell Church Explosion, 2004*).
- How to train future cell leaders (*Leadership Explosion, 2001; Live, 2007; Encounter, 2007; Grow, 2007; Share, 2007; Lead, 2007; Coach, 2008; Discover, 2008*).
- How to coach/care for cell leaders (*How to be a Great Cell Group Coach, 2003; Groups of Twelve, 2000; From Twelve to Three, 2002*).
- How the gifts of the Spirit work within the cell group (*The Spirit-filled Small Group, 2005, 2009; Discover, 2008*).
- How to fine tune your cell system (*Making Cell Groups Work Navigation Guide, 2003*).
- Principles from the second largest church in the world (*Passion and Persistence, 2004*).
- How cell church works in North America (*The Church that Multiplies, 2007, 2009*).
- How to plant a church (*Planting Churches that Reproduce, 2009*)

All of the books listed are available from *Joel Comiskey Group* **by calling toll-free 1-888-511-9995 or by ordering at:**
www.joelcomiskeygroup.com

How To Lead A Great Cell Group Meeting: *So People Want to Come Back*

Do people expectantly return to your group meetings every week? Do you have fun and experience joy during your meetings? Is everyone participating in discussion and ministry? You can lead a great cell group meeting, one that is life changing and dynamic. Most people don't realize that they can create a God-filled atmosphere because they don't know how. Now the secret is out. This guide will show you how to:

- Prepare yourself spiritually to hear God during the meeting
- Structure the meeting so it flows
- Spur people in the group to participate and share their lives openly
- Share your life with others in the group
- Create stimulating questions
- Listen effectively to discover what is transpiring in others' lives
- Encourage and edify group members
- Open the group to non-Christians
- See the details that create a warm atmosphere

By implementing these time-tested ideas, your group meetings will become the hot-item of your members' week. They will go home wanting more and return each week bringing new people with them. 140 pgs.

Home Cell Group Explosion: *How Your Small Group Can Grow and Multiply*

The book crystallizes the author's findings in some eighteen areas of research, based on a meticulous questionnaire that he submitted to cell church leaders in eight countries around the world, locations that he also visited personally for his research. The detailed notes in the back of the book offer the student of cell church growth a rich mine for further reading. The beauty of Comiskey's book is that he not only summarizes his survey results in a thoroughly convincing way but goes on to analyze in practical ways many of his survey results in separate chapters. The happy result is that any cell church leader, intern or member completing this quick read will have his priorities/values clearly aligned and ready to be followed-up. If you are a pastor or small group leader, you should devour this book! It will encourage you and give you simple, practical steps for dynamic small group life and growth. 175 pgs.

An Appointment with the King: *Ideas for Jump-Starting Your Devotional Life*

With full calendars and long lists of things to do, people often put on hold life's most important goal: building an intimate relationship with God. Often, believers wish to pursue the goal but are not sure how to do it. They feel frustrated or guilty when their attempts at personal devotions seem empty and unfruitful. With warm, encouraging writing, Joel Comiskey guides readers on how to set a daily appointment with the King and make it an exciting time they will look forward to. This book first answers the question "Where do I start?" with step-by-step instructions on how to spend time with God and practical ideas for experiencing him more fully. Second, it highlights the benefits of spending time with God, including joy, victory over sin, and spiritual guidance. The book will help Christians tap into God's resources on a daily basis, so that even in the midst of busyness they can walk with him in intimacy and abundance. 175 pgs.

Reap the Harvest: *How a Small Group System Can Grow Your Church*

Have you tried small groups and hit a brick wall? Have you wondered why your groups are not producing the fruit that was promised? Are you looking to make your small groups more effective? Cell-church specialist and pastor Dr. Joel Comiskey studied the world's most successful cell churches to determine why they grow. The key: They have embraced specific principles. Conversely, churches that do not embrace these same principles have problems with their groups and therefore do not grow. Cell churches are successful not because they have small groups but because they can support the groups. In this book, you will discover how these systems work. 236 pgs.

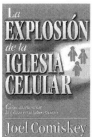

La Explosión de la Iglesia Celular: *Cómo Estructurar la Iglesia en Células Eficaces* (Editorial Clie, 2004)

This book is only available in Spanish and contains Joel Comiskey's research of eight of the world's largest cell churches, five of which reside in Latin America. It details how to make the transition from a traditional church to the cell church structure and many other valuable insights, including: the history of the cell church, how to organize your church to become a praying church, the most important principles of the cell church, and how to raise up an army of cell leaders. 236 pgs.

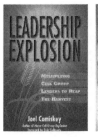

Leadership Explosion: *Multiplying Cell Group Leaders to Reap the Harvest*

Some have said that cell groups are leader breeders. Yet even the best cell groups often have a leadership shortage. This shortage impedes growth and much of the harvest goes untouched. Joel Comiskey has discovered why some churches are better at raising up new cell leaders than others. These churches do more than pray and hope for new leaders. They have an intentional strategy, a plan that will quickly equip as many new leaders as possible. In this book, you will discover the training models these churches use to multiply leaders. You will discover the underlying principles of these models so that you can apply them.
202 pgs.

FIVE-BOOK EQUIPPING SERIES

    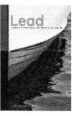

#1: Live   #2: Encounter   #3: Grow   #4: Share   #5: Lead

The five book equipping series is designed to train a new believer all the way to leading his or her own cell group. Each of the five books contains eight lessons. Each lesson has interactive activities that helps the trainee reflect on the lesson in a personal, practical way.

Live starts the training by covering key Christian doctrines, including baptism and the Lord's supper. 85 pgs.

Encounter guides the believer to receive freedom from sinful bondages. The Encounter book can be used one-on-one or in a group. 91 pgs.

Grow gives step-by-step instruction for having a daily quiet time, so that the believer will be able to feed him or herself through spending daily time with God. 87 pgs.

Share instructs the believer how to communicate the gospel message in a winsome, personal way. This book also has two chapters on small group evangelism. 91 pgs.

Lead prepares the Christian on how to facilitate an effective cell group. This book would be great for those who form part of a small group team. 91 pgs.

TWO-BOOK ADVANCED TRAINING SERIES

Coach and Discover make-up the Advanced Training, prepared specifically to take a believer to the next level of maturity in Christ.

Coach prepares a believer to coach another cell leader. Those experienced in cell ministry often lack understanding on how to coach someone else. This book provides step-by-step instruction on how to coach a new cell leader from the first meeting all the way to giving birth to a new group. The book is divided into eight lessons, which are interactive and help the potential coach deal with real-life, practical coaching issues. 85 pgs.

Discover clarifies the twenty gifts of the Spirit mentioned in the New Testament. The second part shows the believer how to find and use his or her particular gift. This book is excellent to equip cell leaders to discover the giftedness of each member in the group. 91 pgs.

How to be a Great Cell Group Coach:
Practical insight for Supporting and Mentoring Cell Group Leaders

Research has proven that the greatest contributor to cell group success is the quality of coaching provided for cell group leaders. Many are serving in the position of a coach, but they don't fully understand what they are supposed to do in this position. Joel Comiskey has identified seven habits of great cell group coaches. These include: Receiving from God, Listening to the needs of the cell group leader, Encouraging the cell group leader, Caring for the multiple aspects of a leader's life, Developing the cell leader in various aspects of leadership, Strategizing with the cell leader to create a plan, Challenging the cell leader to grow.

Practical insights on how to develop these seven habits are outlined in section one. Section two addresses how to polish your skills as a coach with instructions on diagnosing problems in a cell group, how to lead coaching meetings, and what to do when visiting a cell group meeting. This book will prepare you to be a great cell group coach, one who mentors, supports, and guides cell group leaders into great ministry. 139 pgs.

Groups of Twelve: *A New Way to Mobilize Leaders and Multiply Groups in Your Church*

This book clears the confusion about the Groups of 12 model. Joel dug deeply into the International Charismatic Mission in Bogota, Colombia and other G12 churches to learn the simple principles that G12 has to offer your church. This book also contrasts the G12 model with the classic 5x5 and shows you what to do with this new model of ministry. Through onsite research, international case studies, and practical experience, Joel Comiskey outlines the G12 principles that your church can use today.

Billy Hornsby, director of the Association of Related Churches, says, "Joel Comiskey shares insights as a leader who has himself raised up numerous leaders. From how to recognize potential leaders to cell leader training to time-tested principles of leadership--this book has it all. The accurate comparisons of various training models make it a great resource for those who desire more leaders. Great book!" 182 pgs.

From Twelve To Three: *How to Apply G12 Principles in Your Church*

The concept of the Groups of 12 began in Bogota, Colombia, but now it is sweeping the globe. Joel Comiskey has spent years researching the G12 structure and the principles behind it.

From his experience as a pastor, trainer, and consultant, he has discovered that there are two ways to embrace the G12 concept: adopting the entire model or applying the principles that support the model.

This book focuses on the application of principles rather than adoption of the entire model. It outlines the principles and provides a modified application which Joel calls the G12.3. This approach presents a pattern that is adaptable to many different church contexts.

The concluding section illustrates how to implement the G12.3 in various kinds of churches, including church plants, small churches, large churches, and churches that already have cells. 178 pgs.

The Spirit-filled Small Group: *Leading Your Group to Experience the Spiritual Gifts.*
The focus in many of today's small groups has shifted from Spirit-led transformation to just another teacher-student Bible study. But exercising every member's spiritual gifts is vital to the effectiveness of the group. With insight born of experience in more than twenty years of small group ministry, Joel Comiskey explains how leaders and participants alike can be supernaturally equipped to deal with real-life issues. Put these principles into practice and your small group will never be the same!

This book works well with Comiskey's training book, ***Discover.*** It fleshes out many of the principles in Comiskey's training book. Chuck Crismier, radio host, Viewpoint, writes, "Joel Comiskey has again provided the Body of Christ with an important tool to see God's Kingdom revealed in and through small groups." 191 pgs.

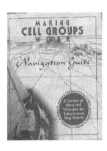

Making Cell Groups Work Navigation Guide: *A Toolbox of Ideas and Strategies for Transforming Your Church.*
For the first time, experts in cell group ministry have come together to provide you with a 600 page reference tool like no other. When Ralph Neighbour, Bill Beckham, Joel Comiskey and Randall Neighbour compiled new articles and information under careful orchestration and in-depth understanding that Scott Boren brings to the table, it's as powerful as private consulting! Joel Comiskey has an entire book within this mammoth 600 page work. There are also four additional authors.

Passion and Persistence: *How the Elim Church's Cell Groups Penetrated an Entire City for Jesus*
This book describes how the Elim Church in San Salvador grew from a small group to 116,000 people in 10,000 cell groups. Comiskey takes the principles from Elim and applies them to churches in North America and all over the world.

Ralph Neighbour says: "I believe this book will be remember as one of the most important ever written about a cell church movement! I experienced the *passion* when visiting Elim many years ago. Comiskey's report about Elim is not a *pattern* to be slavishly copied. It is a journey into grasping the true theology and methodology of the New Testament church. You'll discover how the Elim Church fans into flame their passion for Jesus and His Word, how they organize their cells to penetrate a city and world for Jesus, and how they persist until God brings the fruit."

The Church that Multiplies: *Growing a Healthy Cell Church in North America.*

Does the cell church strategy work in North America? We hear about exciting cell churches in Colombia and Korea, but where are the dynamic North American cell churches? This book not only declares that the cell church concept does work in North America but dedicates an entire chapter to examining North American churches that are successfully using the cell strategy to grow in quality and quantity. This book provides the latest statistical research about the North American church and explains why the cell church approach restores health and growth to the church today. More than anything else, this book will provide practical solutions for pastors and lay leaders to use in implementing cell-based ministry. 181 pgs.

Planting Churches that Reproduce: *Planting a Network of Simple Churchces.*

What is the best way to plant churches in the 21st century? Comiskey believes that simple, reproducible church planting is most effective. The key is to plant churches that are simple enough to grow into a movement of churches. Comiskey has been gathering material for this book for the past fifteen Years. He has also planted three churches in a wide variety of settings. Planting Churches that Reproduce is the fruit of his research and personal experience. Comiskey uses the latest North American church planting statistics, but extends the illustrations to include worldwide church planting. More than anything else, this book will provide practical solutions for those planting churches today. Comiskey's book is a must-read book for all those interested in establishing Christ-honoring, multiplying churches. 176 pgs.

Made in the USA
Middletown, DE
13 January 2019